History of California

A Captivating Guide to the History of the Golden State, Starting from when Native Americans Dominated through European Exploration to the Present

Free Bonus from Captivating History (Available for a Limited time)

Hi History Lovers!

Now you have a chance to join our exclusive history list so you can get your first history ebook for free as well as discounts and a potential to get more history books for free! Simply visit the link below to join.

Captivatinghistory.com/ebook

Also, make sure to follow us on Facebook, Twitter and Youtube by searching for Captivating History.

Contents

Introduction

Although California is known for its many landmarks, such as the Golden Gate Bridge and the Hollywood Sign, and its many famous personalities, it would take many centuries for the state to develop into what it is today, and it wouldn't actually be until 1850 that California was considered an American state at all.

California's earliest history actually dates back to many millennia ago, somewhere between 10,000 and 14,000 years ago. However, these years are far from exact, as it is still a matter of heavy debate amongst experts. Regardless of when the first settlers appeared, there is little debate as to how America's first people arrived. Thousands of years ago, hunters from Asia traveled along a land bridge that connected Asia to Alaska, known as the Bering Strait, while they pursued their prehistoric prey. Over time, these people made it to North America, where they gradually split up and spread out across the continent, eventually making it to California, likely by following the Pacific coast. Unlike the first people in Canada or other states in America, California's first people split off into hundreds and hundreds of smaller groups, as some wanted to settle while others continued to migrate. Over time, California's first people had established tribes all over the state. However, the groups had little contact with each other, which is yet another thing that sets

California's first settlers apart from the first settlers elsewhere in the country. This was mostly due to California's rugged landscape, which made traveling long distances less convenient than in other locations. In addition, the region's expansive wildlife and botany meant less migrating was necessary to find food. Seeing as the region of California is renowned for its diverse landscapes, including but not limited to the rainy redwood forests, Pacific Ocean coastline, the Mojave Desert, the snow-capped Sierra Nevada Mountains, the Central Valley fertile plains, as well as various smaller rivers, lakes, and microenvironments, every tribe quickly adapted their own culture, traditions, and lifestyle, which would have been dependent on their location. Overall, California's first settlers were quite peaceful, mostly since the groups had little contact, which allowed the tribes to truly establish their cultures and systems without violent interruptions. By the 16th century, California's first settlers, who had traveled together across the Bering Strait, split into more than 500 tribes spread throughout the region of California, with around 135 distinct unique dialects.

As the Native Americans in California established their cultures, the rest of the Americas were slowly being discovered over the course of the 15th and 16th centuries. Although the Spaniards would not actually make any moves to colonize California until the 18th century, California is believed to have received its name in the early 16th century. While there is some debate as to the true origin of the state's name, the most common origin story is that the name came from the fictional novel *Las Sergas de Esplandián* (*The Adventures of Esplandián*), written by Spanish author Garci Rodríguez de Montalvo. The romantic thriller was set on an island with sandy soil and hidden gold and riches. The island was located to the right of the Indies, referring to Southeast Asia. Although California is not an island and the Spaniards had no idea of the region's gold at the time, even before the Europeans first discovered California in 1542, they referred to the landmass north of Mexico as the island of California. As the

Spaniards explored what would eventually become the Gulf of California, it was later discovered that California was, in fact, a peninsula attached to a far larger landmass. Over the course of the early 1500s, California would slowly be discovered as the Spaniards slowly explored and claimed the areas near their colony of Mexico; however, the region would remain completely untouched by the Europeans until the 1700s, leaving the Native Americans in California to continue to develop their culture and grow their population. It is estimated that by the 18th century, there were somewhere between 300,000 and 700,000 Native Americans in the region of California.

By the 18th century, while the United States of America had already begun its revolution, the Spaniards finally returned to California in order to explore and colonize the region that they had claimed centuries beforehand. The main reasons for Spain's renewed interest in California were that missionaries wanted to convert the region's native population and that Spain feared other countries might try to claim the land as their own, Russia being the primary threat, as they hunted otters in Alaska and began pursuing them down the Pacific coastline, just as the Native Americans had done millennia before. In 1769, Spanish explorers, led by Gaspar de Portolá, set sail from Mexico and began the journey of colonizing California. Though the route was hazardous and the maps were faulty, the boats finally reached California and arrived in present-day San Diego. Three months after arriving, Father Junípero Serra, who had been on one of the ships, created California's first mission, and he began making contact with the Native Americans so he could begin converting the tribes to Christianity. The tribes, who had lived uninterruptedly for thousands of years, establishing their own religions, cultures, and lifestyles, were given little choice, as they were often forced with violence to convert to Christianity. However, the missionary movement did not enforce only the Christian religion but also the European colonial way of living. The Native Americans would be forced to live in cramped walled enclosures even if they already had established villages nearby and were promptly taught Spanish along with many traditional European working skills, such as blacksmithing and brickmaking. Over the next thirty years, Mission San Diego would establish extensive European-inspired irrigation systems, which would aid the Native Americans in their forced labor of cultivating tens of thousands of acres. Although the Native Americans worked to cultivate the land and create a surplus of food, they reaped no rewards, as the food went to feed the European settlers. Any excess was exchanged with Mexico, allowing the Spaniards to acquire luxury items.

Over the next few years, Gaspar de Portolá and Junípero Serra continued to establish their presence in California; however, colonization did not really take place until after 1773. The small group who had arrived by boat in California was hardly enough to establish a European presence in the region, and the Spaniards in Mexico and Spain were not keen to embark on another long journey through the Pacific's hazardous waters to reach California. The land was not much safer either, and with California's deserts and rugged landscape, no European had managed to find a safe passage between Mexico and California, but that would change when the task was given to Juan Bautista de Anza. In 1774, with the help of the Native Americans, Anza discovered a safe path to California, and the next year, he led 240 men, women, and children, this time along with 700 horses and mules and around 350 cattle, to California, where they formed the city of San Francisco. The Spaniards had managed to create California's first real cities while at the same time reducing the Native American population by over 100,000 people. However, by the 19th century, California would no longer be theirs to colonize at all.

Just as the United States had gained its freedom from Britain in 1776, Mexico gained its independence from Spain in 1821, and while gaining its freedom, the newly created Republic of Mexico acquired California. Mexico promptly drove out the Spanish missionaries and parceled up the missionary land into land grants, which were known as ranchos. These land grants, given to a number of well-liked Mexican and Spanish civilians, created the first elite businessmen in California, which had previously been run by the church. Although the Native American population was freed from the missionaries, many of them ended up working as serfs on the Californian ranchos, their situation only mildly improved. Although the Mexican hold on California was way less strong than the Spanish church's was in the years before, Californians were not pleased with the new systems set in place by the Republic of Mexico, and public resentment started growing. During the period of Mexican California, the United States gradually increased its own interest in acquiring the region, and immigrants arrived from all over the country, which only added to the already growing Californian hostility toward Mexico. Following the 1846 Bear Flag Revolt, where a small group of Americans raised the first iteration of California's state flag and declared California's independence from Mexico, the United States and Mexico entered into war with each other over the state of California, among other issues. Finally, on February 2nd, 1848, the Mexican-American War ended, and California officially became a part of the United States, although they would have to wait to achieve statehood until they reached a minimum of 60,000 people.

At the end of the war, California had a fairly small population, and it seemed as if it could be at least a decade before California acquired statehood. However, they would blow past the 60,000 people requirement and achieve statehood in 1850. The reason for this incredible increase in population was the discovery of gold near present-day Sacramento, just as the Garci Rodríguez de Montalvo novel, *Las Sergas de Esplandián* (*The Adventures of Esplandián*), had predicted. Although the gold was discovered nine days before the end of the Mexican-American War, word would not actually reach the United States or the rest of the world until months later. However, Californians found out quite quickly, and they lined the hills near the river where the gold had been found with temporary tents and wooden huts. By 1849, the Gold Rush had officially begun, and people came from all over the world to try and strike it rich in California's gold mines. Over the course of 1849, it is estimated around 80,000 people, known as forty-niners, arrived in California. The following year, after some debates, California earned its statehood. The Gold Rush essentially birthed California's economy, as many who arrived in California pretty quickly realized that amongst all of the competition, one would actually be more successful if they set up businesses around the Gold Rush rather than mining for gold themselves. By the end of the Gold Rush, more than 300,000 people had permanently emigrated to California, which forced California to expand its cities and internal farming and manufacturing. As a result, a local economy developed quickly, and California became attractive to even those who were not interested in the Gold Rush at all.

The California Gold Rush would help fund the Union during the American Civil War, and by the end of the war, the United States realized the importance of its newly acquired state and the disadvantage of it not being connected to the rest of the United States. The end of the Civil War brought about the transcontinental railway, which, in turn, brought about another mass immigration to California. The expansion of Southern California, which at that point had remained mostly inhabited by the Native Americans, was also encouraged, and the new settlers promptly pushed the natives out of their land. By the end of the 19th century, California would be a diverse, multicultural society, with its own booming local economy and nothing but growth on the forefront.

By 1900, the population of California had grown to well over a million people, and the economy continued to flourish, even though almost all of the state's gold had been excavated at that point. New industries opened up every decade when the demands changed. For instance, California's suburbs grew with the automobile and oil industry boom, and California's weapon and aircraft manufacturing industries were born when the United States joined World War I. Although there were serious recessions, most notably the 1929 crash, which would bring about the Great Depression, California's economy always found a way to not only recover but also grow astronomically in the process. World War II would be, in many ways, a second gold rush for California, as millions would flock to the state for jobs.

Although the mass immigration to California was positive for the state's economy, it was not beneficial to all, especially in regards to the Native American population, who would be forced onto reservations, often in other states. As the population of California boomed, it quickly became one of the most multicultural states in the country, which was not without its own issues. While the white Americans prospered in California's economy, there was little upward mobility for foreigners or even racial minorities who had been citizens of California for decades at this point. With the growth of the economy came the growth of the divide between the rich and the poor that had started in Mexican California's rancho days. California would quickly become home to protests, rallies, and various social movements. Although the state had almost always been primarily Republican, by the end of the 20th century, California would become one of the most diverse, left-leaning, progressive states in the country, and by the 21st century, the protests, rallies, and various social movements over the years brought other openminded people to the state, transforming California into a major Democratic state.

Chapter 1 – Early History and the Arrival of America's First People (Year Unknown–1542)

In 1492, Italian explorer Christopher Columbus claimed the land he discovered in the Americas for Spain, but by this point in history, there were already many communities of people who inhabited the land and had done so for thousands of years. The first people of California were not Italian like Christopher Columbus nor Spaniards; in fact, they were not any type of European at all. Instead, they had come from Asia and traveled along a land bridge that no longer exists on the Arctic and Pacific Oceans. This ancient bridge, known as the Bering Strait, is believed to have been mostly grassy wetlands, but as water levels rose, the land was covered up by the water that connects Siberia to what is now Alaska. Regardless of whether the Bering Strait was land at the time or as it is now, a frozen bridge, the first people of America made quite a trip, seeing as the narrowest distance between mainland Russia and America today is around eighty-eight kilometers (fifty-five miles). What made this trip, which was done on foot, possible was the warmer climate and the access to food, and although historians are not too sure of the vegetation of the Bering Strait, the travelers had at least the meat of the prey they were hunting.

Although few experts debate that California's first people originated from Asia and arrived in America after hunting and following woolly mammoths, steppe bison, and other prehistoric mammals across the Bering Strait, when exactly they arrived is a point of contention amongst most historians and experts. The most common belief is that America's first people set foot in America sometime between 10,000 and 20,000 years ago and gradually spread across North America until eventually reaching what is now California, Baja California, and South America. However, a controversial discovery made at Cerutti Mastodon, a paleontological and archaeological site located in San Diego County, California, contradicts that common opinion. In 1992, during the construction of California's State Route 54, the team of construction workers manning the excavator dug up more than just dirt and rocks from the ground. The workers discovered large bone fragments on the site, which upon further digging also contained the skeleton of a mastodon, bone flakes, and several large stones. It is believed that the location was used by ancient humans sometime between 120,000 and 140,000 years ago as a "bone quarry," where the people would have used stone hammers to smash mastodon bones in order to use the material. This would, of course, place the first people in America over one hundred thousand years before the commonly believed date of their arrival. It took paleontologists and archaeologists until 2011 to actually place the date of the site, which was accomplished with the help of the trace amounts of uranium and thorium found within the mastodon bones. Seeing as it took the experts so long to date the site, and since the data is not entirely reliable, accurate, or foolproof, there is still much contention as to the actual date of arrival of America's first people. Many historians would rather stick to the more proven period between 10,000 and 20,000 years ago until further proof comes out saying otherwise.

Regardless of when the Asian settlers first stepped foot in America, it is known that the group began splitting into more distinct tribes and nations while gradually spreading throughout what is now Canada, the United States, and eventually South America. What makes the first people of California unique from the other native peoples of the Americas are the sheer number of different nations and tribes within the state, which all have their own unique culture, traditions, and lifestyle. This is due to California's diverse landscapes and habitats, which still exist within the state today. As the nations continued splitting up and spreading throughout California's vast land, they developed their own lifestyles based on the landscape around them. Some adapted sedentary agricultural lifestyles, while others were nomads and depended on hunting and gathering for sustenance. Since the small tribes became isolated in their unique environments, they developed their own distinct dialects, traditions, and cultures, which differed immensely from their closest neighbors. It is estimated that the original first people of America, who traveled together across the Bering Strait, split into more than 500 tribes spread throughout the state of California and gave birth to around 135 distinct unique dialects.

What greatly aided in solidifying the diversity of America's first people was California's rugged, difficult-to-traverse landscape, which isolated the individual tribes from one another. Although the nations were familiar with traveling rugged land, seeing as they had traversed much of the Pacific coast of North America by the time they had reached California, once the nations settled in their respective homes, they tended to stay within the area. Seeing as the state of California is ideal for various types of flora and fauna, there were far fewer nomad nations than in the rest of North America, and the tribes that were nomadic did not have to travel as far to find food. What this means is that there was far less interaction between the diverse tribes of California and that there was also little warfare, especially when compared to early tribes in other states. Overall, the first tribes of

California experienced relatively peaceful lives, allowing them to develop more elaborate and complex systems and cultures than tribes undergoing destructive and distracting wars. The only outside interaction many of these people had was with neighboring tribes, who, due to proximity, likely shared some cultural commonalities. Of course, they also often engaged in the trade of goods and services with each other. These abnormally peaceful trading systems allowed California's first settlers to further diversify and develop their material objects. Seeing as California's tribes were so small and tight-knit, there was little need for strict political structures, unlike the larger nations in the rest of America.

Seeing as each individual nation developed in relative isolation, a tribe in the north of California would bear almost no cultural resemblances to a tribe in the south of California. That being said, seeing as an entire book can be written on any one of the distinctively unique tribes alone, grouping the hundreds and hundreds of tribes of California's early settlers into categories based on landscape and location will only allow for a small insight into the interesting cultures and diversity amongst the native Californians. Seeing as the neighboring tribes did share some cultural similarities, simply based on their shared landscape and communication, historians often group together California's tribes into the following categories: Northeastern tribes, Northwestern tribes, Central tribes, and Southern tribes.

Northeastern Tribes

Much like the rest of California, the landscape in northeastern California is extremely varied, and there are hundreds of different unique tribes that inhabit this region of the state. That being said, some of the more debatably "notable" tribes include the Modoc, Achumawi, and Atsugewi. The Achumawi or Achomawi tribes were located between Big Bend to Goose Lake, farther to the east in the northeastern region. The nation became known as river people, as their diet was extremely dependent on fishing, more so than other tribes. The Atsugewi tribes, who had trade relations and communication with the Achumawi tribes, resided mostly around Mount Shasta, which is one of the highest peaks in California. The group, as well as other tribes in the area, became known as the "Pit River Indians" due to the pits that were dug in and around the local creeks to make catching game easier. The Atsugewi and the Achumawi not only had trade connections but, seeing as their communities were located not too far away, also often had similar diets, which included berries, deer, rabbit, grass seeds, and tule. Many of the tribes in the eastern region of northeastern California also took advantage of the abundance of tule, which is an aquatic plant, by not only eating it but also lacing it together to create floor mats. The Modoc tribe, who today no longer inhabit California (as they have moved to Oregon and Oklahoma), may be one of the state's most well-known tribes due to the intense wars that would later happen against the United States military in the late 19th century. Prior to the arrival of Europeans, the Modoc tribe was scattered throughout northeastern California, seeing as they migrated seasonally to hunt and gather. During the winter months, they would stay sedentary in beehive-shaped, semi-underground lodgings built from wood and mud.

Of course, there were many more tribes who inhabited and still inhabit the northeastern region of California, including some who harvested obsidian for trade from the state's volcanic mountains. The obsidian was sharpened by any tribe who could get their hands on it to create ceremonial items, knives, hunting weapons, and, later on, weapons for war. Since volcanic glass is extremely sharp and strong, it became quite the sought-after commodity.

Northwestern Tribes

Similar to the northeastern region of California, there are many different landscapes, climates, and environments to the west that were inhabited by hundreds of tribes, each with its own distinctive culture and dialects. Some of the more well-known northwestern tribes include the Tolowa, Shasta, Karok, Yurok Hupa Whilikut, Chilula,

Chimarike, and Wiyot tribes, and similarly to the Modoc tribe out east, many of these nations were made known due to their involvement in what are known as the American Indian Wars in the late 19th century. Northwestern California is known for its redwood forests and the Pacific coast, as well as some mountains, lagoons, bays, rivers, and other waterways. Many of the northwestern tribes took advantage of the dense redwood forests at their disposal and used the lumber to build homes, which they constructed using a rectangular gabled design. Seeing as the tribes were taking down monstrous trees, which, when matured, have an average height of 200 to 240 feet, a lot of cutting was necessary to not only fell the massive trees but also to separate the lumber into manageable pieces. Since the tribes didn't have many of the effective tools we have today for taking down trees, they would actually burn the bases and then chop the tree down and split it up with elkhorn wedges. Although the tribes did traverse through the redwood forests on foot to cut down trees, their main way of travel and transport was by canoes, which they also built with the redwood lumber. Seeing as the northwest of California is littered with different waterways, many of which lead back to the Pacific Ocean, traveling by boat was the most efficient means of travel. The tribes of the northwest generally established their villages along the waterways, which made trade and relations between tribes more common than with those to the east, who were separated by rugged terrain.

The people who inhabited the northwest region of California suffered through many food deprivations and natural disasters, specifically earthquakes and floods, something that the people of California still deal with to this day. To ward off the many potential disasters that plagued the people inhabiting the region, many tribes had their own unique traditions, ceremonies, and rituals, which they practiced whether the community was lacking food or not. Furthermore, the northwestern tribes had their own unique artistry and craftsmanship traditions, which can best be seen in their basket making. The northwestern tribes are known for their twined baskets, which stand out against the baskets of other tribes who had access to different crafting materials. Another difference between the northwestern tribes and many other native nations of America is that the northwestern tribes had a clear hierarchy where lineage mattered, and those at the top would have more access to wealth, which, in their time, was the private ownership of bountiful food resources.

Central Tribes

Central California is a vaguely drawn-out large territory in the center of the state, which contains so many different landscapes, environments, and, of course, Native American nations. Some of the more well-known tribes who inhabit the Pacific coast, valleys, and mountain ranges in central California include the Pomo and Miwok nations, but, of course, these two barely scratch the surface. The Pomo tribe is well known today due to their coiled and twine baskets, which are elaborately designed with intricate color shifts and pattern work, which appear more like works of art than functional containers. The Pomo nation is also well known due to their proximity to what is now the city of San Francisco. The Pomo are known for their practice of the Kuksu religion, which is a Native American religion shared amongst a few northern and centralized nations in California. Traditionally, those who practice Kuksu have very specific ceremonies that are practiced to ensure good fortune in harvests, fertility, and other important matters.

The Miwok, who are spread all over central California, still has a larger population than most of the other nations in California. Within just the Miwok nation, there were seven distinct dialects and cultures, and by the time of European contact, the tribe had spread into over a hundred separate small villages. As with the rest of the Native Americans, even those outside California, every Miwok tribe established and developed their own unique customs and lifestyle based on where they were living, how many people were in the tribe, and other factors. The Miwok tribes located close to the coast lived in partially underground earth and pole-covered lodgings, and they gathered acorns, fished, and hunted deer and small game with bow and arrows. The Plains and Sierra Miwok, who were also known as the interior Miwok, lived in semi-subterranean earth-covered lodgings. When they hunted in the mountains, which they did in the warmer months, they would live in quickly assembled temporary lean-to lodgings. Like the Pomo nation, many of the interior Miwok tribes actively practiced Kuksu.

Although other tribes in the centralized region had their own systems and traditions, their general proximity in location means many of them shared some lifestyle elements. Whether in the mountains or on the coast, the tribes in central California were mostly hunter-gatherer groups who generally enjoyed an abundance of food such as acorns, deer, rabbit, elk, antelope, and salmon. Throughout central California, the semi-subterranean home was quite popular, although different tribes had different coverings depending on the available materials. Furthermore, the central tribes in the state were usually very spiritual. Religion was not limited to the followers of Kuksu, as many tribes had their own practices and customs to pray for good fortunes and to remember the patterns of renewal in the world and the circle of life.

Southern Tribes

Seeing as the territory of Southern California covers such a large expanse of land, with some of the most diverse environments in the whole state, including deserts and small islands, it is best to divide the region up into smaller sections to fully grasp the different tribes who settled here. In the north of Southern California, there are many tribes, including the Luiseno Cahuilla, the Kitanemuk, and, likely the most well-known tribe in California, the Chumash.

The Chumash are one of the most well-known nations in the state due to the fact that they were one of the first tribes that the Spaniards had contact with in the early 16th century. Although the Chumash people had a significantly larger population than many of the other tribes in California, some with over a thousand people, they were not as spread out as the similarly large Miwok tribes and instead were all centered around the Channel Islands. Since the tribe lived on various islands, they used double-oared canoes known as tomols, which were designed to carry hundreds if not thousands of pounds of goods and passengers. With their advantage of being surrounded by water and their art of constructing efficient boats, the Chumash often traveled to the other islands and to the main landmass to buy, sell, and trade using clamshell beads as a form of currency. The Chumash people were more than just skilled boat makers, for the tribe has also become known for their skilled artisans, who created wooden tools, intricate baskets, and soapstone sculptures. They established their villages on the water and lived in quite large dome-shaped homes, fashioned with many rooms that they shared with various members of their family. Seeing as the tribes lived on the water, one of their main sources of sustenance was fish, along with other sea animals. Like many of the tribes in California, the Chumash nation relied a great deal on gathering acorns. The reason acorns are not a commonly eaten nut today is due to the fact that they contain a lot of bitter tannins, which can be toxic if consumed in large amounts. However, the Chumash tribes found ways to leach the acorns of their bitter taste and toxicity and made them a staple in their diet. In contrast to their large populations of a thousand people or more in the Channel Islands, the Chumash communities in the desert in southeast California were often as small as 100 people.

The Cahuilla and Serrano were two separate groups that were spread throughout the south of the state, but both had villages in the Southern Californian deserts. To protect from extreme sun and heat, the people would build their homes in conical shapes with whatever materials they had native to their location, such as tule or arrow weed. Seeing as there was little European travel through the Californian desert, and since the desert native tribes were usually quite small, not much is known about the early people who established themselves in these harsh, hot conditions. That being said, traditions such as basket making, clay pottery, tattooing, sandstone carving, and more have been passed down through generations and give some indication as to how the early people might have lived.

Generally, it seems that the Southern Californian tribes shared many practices and systems, such as the naming of a chieftain, the belief in the village's shaman, and the separation of tribes into social classes.

The Native Americans before the Arrival of the Europeans

Although the United States' native population has been there for at least 10,000 years, some would say even 100,000 years, not much is known about their history for certain. Most of what we understand about America's first people comes from archaeological discoveries that line up with European historical accounts, current Native American traditions, and their history that has been passed down through word of mouth for generations. Although we attempted to summarize the Native Americans by geographical region in California, many of the villages that were near each other had very few similarities in customs, traditions, and rituals. After thousands of years of evolution and developing their own culture, they might as well have become a different race, and yet, seeing as they all arrived together, they are grouped together. The differences in lodgings perfectly demonstrate how differently the tribes lived. There were semi-subterranean earth-covered homes, dome-shaped dwellings, cone-shaped desert lodges, wood houses, large multi-room family homes, small nomadic hunting tents, and temporary lean-to homes. Some tribes traveled on foot, while others did so by boat. Unfortunately, most of the native tribes that are known today are only known due to their casinos, their mistreatment by the Europeans, and the wars with the Americans later in history. Yet, they had hundreds of unique cultures that existed far before Europeans claimed America. Upon the Spaniards' arrival in California in 1542, there were around 130,000 Native Americans in what is now defined as the state of California, but so much is still unknown about the peoples that lived in the United States before the 16th-century arrival of the Europeans.

Chapter 2 – Origin of California's Name and the First European Exploration (1510–1602)

Eighteen years after Christopher Columbus sailed the Atlantic Ocean and set foot in the Americas in 1492, on what is now recognized as the Bahamas, and three years before Juan Ponce de León became the first European to set foot in the United States of America in 1513, California is believed to have received its name. Although there is some debate as to whether the true origin of California's name is, in fact, from the Native Americans or the Europeans, the most popular opinion is that the name originates from a fictional novel titled *Las Sergas de Esplandián* (*The Adventures of Esplandián.*) The romantic thriller, written by Spanish writer Garci Rodríguez de Montalvo, was published in 1510, some five years after the author's death, meaning the future name of the state was likely conceptualized many years before 1505. The novel follows the adventures of the mythical and beautiful Amazonian queen and warrior, Calafia, who, accompanied by her pet griffin, ruled over an island of woman. Garci Rodríguez de

Montalvo described Queen Calafia's island to have sandy soil and hidden gold and riches. This island paradise described in *Las Sergas de Esplandián* was named California. Whether the name truly originates from Garci Rodríguez de Montalvo's novel is, of course, unknown; however, it was the first written appearance of the name California, and seeing as the novel had been somewhat popular in Spain before the Spanish set foot in what would eventually become California, it makes sense that the name could have come from *Las Sergas de Esplandián.*

One year after Garci Rodríguez de Montalvo's novel was published, the Spanish explorer Vasco Núñez de Balboa became the first European to spot the Pacific shoreline. Although he did not technically set foot in California or anywhere on the Pacific coast, while exploring Panama in 1513, which the travelers reached from the Atlantic Ocean, Vasco Núñez de Balboa is said to have climbed a mountain and spotted the Pacific Ocean. The same year, the Spanish explorer Juan Ponce de León became the first European to set foot in the United States of America after settling in Puerto Rico and sailing to Florida.

In 1519, the Spaniards began their conquest of Mexico, and in 1521, Hernán Cortés officially defeated the Aztecs and succeeded in conquering Mexico. Following his conquest in Mexico, the Spaniard continued exploring both the Gulf of Mexico, which would lead him to Honduras, and the Pacific coast of Mexico. As he began aging, Hernán Cortés stopped leading expeditions and began commissioning other explorers to fulfill his curiosity. It would be one of his commissioned explorers, Francisco de Ulloa, who would lead the exploration of the Gulf of California, which he named the Sea of Cortés in 1539. Francisco de Ulloa's explorations in the late 1530s detailed that California was, in fact, a peninsula, although it would be years until this would be seen as a fact since it was still commonly believed that the land to the northwest of Mexico was an island.

During Francisco de Ulloa's expeditions, he also discovered the Colorado River.

In 1540, after Francisco de Ulloa's discovery, explorer Hernando de Alarcón was sent to sail the Colorado River. By this point, the Europeans were aware of Baja California, but it was not until Hernando de Alarcón's expedition that any European had seen Alta California, which refers to the upper region of the state. In the early 16ᵗʰ century, the explorers were still unsure as to whether California was an island or a peninsula, nor did they have any idea that the state was attached to a much larger continent. However, seeing as no one had actually set foot in California as of yet, the landmass was referred to as the island of California. In the summer of 1542, Spanish explorer Juan Rodríguez Cabrillo set off from the Mexican port of Navidad on an expedition through the Gulf of California (then the Sea of Cortés) to the Colorado River. Cabrillo and his crew are said to have first set foot in the state of California, which they named Alta California, on September 28ᵗʰ, 1542. They explored San Diego and the Monterey Bays, which made them the first Europeans to not only set foot in what is now the state of California but also the first to have contact with the native Californians. Juan Rodríguez Cabrillo estimated there were likely more than 100,000 Native Americans living in California upon his arrival in 1542.

Subsequent to Juan Rodríguez Cabrillo's official discovery of California, Spain began focusing on the exploration and colonization of the Philippines, which distracted them from further exploring California. Regardless of the Spanish Empire's plans in the Philippines, there was a general decline in Spanish explorations toward the end of the 16ᵗʰ century, which meant that California remained mostly untouched by the Europeans until the latter half of the 18ᵗʰ century. In 1602, Spanish explorer Sebastián Vizcaíno set sail from Mexico, alongside multiple vessels, to California, and after over half a year of travel, they reached San Diego. The city of San Diego, which had been previously named San Miguel by Juan Rodríguez

Cabrillo, was renamed San Diego by Sebastián Vizcaíno after the feast day of San Diego de Alcalá, which was to be celebrated two days after the group's arrival (the European feast is celebrated on November 12th). Sebastián Vizcaíno and his ships continued exploring, reaching Santa Catalina Island and sailing through the Santa Barbara Channel until entering the harbor at Carmel Bay. Although Sebastián Vizcaíno did not technically explore much more than Juan Rodríguez Cabrillo had many decades before, Vizcaíno named some of California's ports and cities (mostly after religious names or after his Spanish leadership) and helped to draw up much more accurate maps than what the Europeans were previously using, which would be depended upon until the late 18th century.

Chapter 3 – First European Settlement and Contact with the Native Population (1769–1821)

California before the Arrival of the Spanish in 1769

What would later become the state of California remained completely untouched by the Europeans for the next century and a half, which allowed the Native American population to grow and their culture to develop uninterrupted. From later mission records, archaeological records of villages, and various censuses conducted over the years, historians estimate the native population in California before the return of the Spaniards in the latter half of the 18th century was somewhere between 130,000 and 1,500,000. Seeing as the native population in California was so spread out, it is impossible to determine an exact number; however, the most specific estimation is that the native population was somewhere between 300,000 and 700,000.

Just before the Europeans set off to once again explore and colonize California, the rest of the United States of America, which then only included thirteen colonies located along the eastern seaboard, were about to head into the revolutionary era. In 1765, the

British Parliament attempted to enact the Stamp Act, which was supposed to raise tax costs on stamps in order to raise the monarchy's revenue. The colonies were far from pleased by this new act and began protesting, rioting, burning stamps, and refusing to use stamps at all. There was much that went behind what set off the American Revolutionary War, but the fact the colonists had no representation in British Parliament is considered one of the prime issues. The American Revolution would officially begin in 1775. However, as the American revolutionaries began to defend their freedoms from British rule, California was only just being discovered and colonized. One of the reasons for the renewed Spanish interest in exploring California after leaving it untouched for over a century was that missionaries had been impatiently waiting and pushing to begin converting the Native Americans. Spain was also encouraged to return to California due to the European demand for sea otter pelts, which were originally found in the Alaskan Aleutian Islands but were hunted and driven south by the Russians. The third reason behind the sudden decision to resume exploration of California was the search for the Northwest Passage, a sea route that connected the Atlantic Ocean to the Pacific Ocean (this wouldn't be discovered by Europeans until the 19th century, though).

The Spaniards Set Sail in 1769

In 1769, Spain's viceroy sent explorers, which were to be led by Gaspar de Portolá, to begin the colonization of California. Gaspar de Portolá, a Spanish nobleman and soldier who was appointed governor of Las Californias in 1767, was instructed to set up bases in Alta California after being ordered to expel the Jesuits from Baja California. Three ships departed under Gaspar de Portolá's lead on their way to California. Seeing as the group was using faulty maps drawn up by Sebastián Vizcaíno in 1602, the voyage was far from peaceful. The group not only dealt with navigational errors that put them months off their route but also heavy winds and storms that they had not been expecting. Many of the men on the ships fell ill and died, and an entire boat of supplies was lost at sea. However, after months of difficulties, on April 11ᵗʰ, the first ship of men arrived in San Diego. On that ship was Father Junípero Serra, who would lead the Christian missionary movement in California over the subsequent years. Junípero Serra, who was later beatified, had entered the Franciscan Order in 1730, and after many years of teaching philosophy, he boarded a ship to Mexico in 1750 and was heavily involved in the missionary movement in Mexico until 1767. After embarking on the expedition led by Gaspar de Portolá, Father Junípero Serra arrived in California, eager to make contact with the Native Americans so he could begin converting the nations to Christianity.

Europeans Arrive in California

On July 16ᵗʰ, 1769, only three months after arriving in San Diego, Junípero Serra established Mission San Diego. Although the Native Americans who inhabited California had established their own religions, culture, and lifestyles, once the Spanish missionaries arrived, they were given little choice in their life. The Spanish Franciscans enforced not only Christianity on the Native Americans, who were known as the neophytes or converts, but also the European colonial way of living. The European missionary movement involved building walled enclosures, where the Native Americans would be forced to live, even if they already had established villages nearby. The converts were taught Spanish along with many traditional European working skills, such as blacksmithing and brickmaking, which they were forced to continue using even after they converted to Christianity, which was done almost always against their will.

Father Junípero Serra's treatment of the native population is of great debate. Although he was, of course, a leading force in the missionary actions in California, he is said to have been less harsh toward the native population than other colonizers. Regardless of how he treated the Native Americans, Mission San Diego was only the first mission of twenty-one set up by Junípero Serra and his successors.

The site for Mission San Diego was chosen not only due to its proximity to the port where the explorers' ship docked but also due to its proximity to multiple Native American villages. Father Serra's choice was well placed, as it had easy access to water and was on fertile land, which was necessary, seeing as one element of the missionary conversion process was to enforce European agriculture systems such as traditional vegetable gardens. Over the next thirty years, Mission San Diego would establish extensive European-inspired irrigation systems, which would aid the Native Americans in cultivating tens of thousands of acres.

Around the same time as the establishment of Mission San Diego, Gaspar de Portolá set up the Presidio of San Diego, which was the first permanent European settlement in not only California but also along the Pacific coast. From there, Gaspar de Portolá, Junípero Serra, and various explorers set out on expeditions throughout California in order to set up more missions and presidios (a fortified settlement or military post). In May of 1770, Gaspar de Portolá established the Presidio of Monterey to act as a military base, which the Spaniards felt was necessary due to the Russian threat, which was one of the main reasons Spain suddenly rushed to colonize California. The Russians, who were actively exploring to find the Northwest Passage and hunting otters, seemed as if they were going to make their way down the Pacific coast. The Spanish did not want to encounter the powerhouse without having established some military bases first. Around a month later, Father Junípero Serra established the Mission Monterey, which would later be relocated and become known as the Mission San Carlos Borromeo de Carmelo.

Over the next few years, Gaspar de Portolá and Junípero Serra continued to establish their presence in Alta California, and explorers also reached San Francisco Bay, which is just around 500 miles on land from where San Diego lays. However, colonization did not really take place until after 1773. During the years prior to 1773, Junípero Serra disputed with the Spanish authorities over how Alta California should be run and colonized, and finally, in 1773, he caused the officials to increase financial and military support in California. To begin properly populating the European settlements, the Spanish officials needed to find a safer way to reach the bases in California since the naval route taken by Portolá was not safe for civilians. Though those who had already settled in Alta California had spent some time exploring the area, all of the land passages seemed to be far too hazardous, both because of the unfamiliar and exhausting desert and mountain terrain and because of the threat that could come from crossing through indigenous nations' land. Junípero Serra, who had acquired a great deal of power in California, had been urging the Spanish officials to establish a land route. Regardless of Serra's pleas, Spain knew it needed to find a safe and reliable way to link the various settlements in Mexico and California, as well as those in today's Arizona and New Mexico. With the threat of Russian invasion to the north and rumors of English exploration that could perhaps reach California, Spanish officials felt pressured to immediately begin populating the resource-filled state with both livestock and settlers, which meant they needed to secure a route and fast.

The assignment of finding a safe passage was given to Juan Bautista de Anza, who, having European Spanish ancestors and blood, was born and raised in Mexico and had spent years fighting in various wars as a frontier commander. In January of 1774, Juan Bautista de Anza finally set out on his journey to find a safe passage to California from Tubac, a town located in present-day Arizona, just under twenty-five miles from the Mexican border. Anza led thirty-four men through the dismally hot and dry deserts in present-day Arizona and California and managed to survive due to help from various native nations along the way, namely the Yuma and Cochimí.

Within only a few months, in March, Juan Bautista de Anza and his crew reached Mission San Gabriel, located only ten miles from modern-day Los Angeles. Mission San Gabriel had been established in 1771, making it the fourth mission established in California at the time. Although the group was exhausted after their more than 500-mile trip, the explorers spent the next few months traveling to Monterey, arriving there in May, which added over an extra 300 miles to their journey. Seeing as Juan Bautista de Anza was not just trying to arrive in the Californian settlements but also map out a secure route, it is estimated that the group traveled over 1,000 miles in five months. The group took their own route back to Tubac, perfecting the trail so they could lead civilians and cattle as soon as possible.

Juan Bautista de Anza was approved for a new expedition, and he departed on his next journey around a year later in October of 1775, but this time, he was accompanied by far more than just thirty-four men. Anza led an estimated 240 people who had been living in northern Mexico, including men, women, and children. Alongside the settlers were close to 700 horses and mules and around 350 cattle. After at least three months of travel, the group arrived in San Gabriel, and three months later, in March of 1776, they briefly stopped in Monterey. The large group continued on their journey to develop a new settlement, and by the end of the month, Anza had established the Presidio of San Francisco. Although Anza and his men had spent close to a year searching for the best trail to California, his journey with the 240 civilians would be the final large journey across this path for close to 100 years. After the Yumi revolt in 1781, the Europeans were forced to avoid their territory. A year later, in 1777, Anza's second-in-command, José Joaquín Moraga, led some of the civilians who had set up in San Francisco to central California and established the Pueblo of San José, which made it the first Spaniard-only town in Alta California.

During this time, Junípero Serra and his associates continued establishing missions. Due to the limited accessibility of California, the Spanish population remained quite small, especially in comparison to the Native American population and the booming American cities on the eastern coast. Despite this, the Native American population was farming enough food to sustain a large city. As part of the missionary process, the neophytes (converts) were taught various agricultural skills, including cattle, grain, olive, wine, and brandy farming and manufacturing. This massive surplus of food allowed the Spanish population to trade with Mexico, allowing the civilians some luxury items, to which early settlements are not usually privy. However, this wealth did not come without a cost, and in this case, it was at the expense of the Native American population. Many thousands of Native Americans were forced to convert to Christianity, and although the native villages often outnumbered the traveling missionaries, the "recruits" were often singled out or followed when alone and then forced to convert, sometimes at gunpoint. To be converted, the Native Americans were baptized, and once baptized, they were essentially bound to the Franciscans' authority. The neophytes worked hard, long hours, adapting to the European agricultural system, which created a surplus of food, but the converts reaped none of the benefits. If a converted Native American disobeyed the Franciscans' authority, it was the law that they could and likely would be whipped or imprisoned. Although the Native American population had established villages and ways of living for thousands of years before the arrival of the Europeans, those who converted were forced into overpopulated walled communities, and they would be hunted down and forced to return or killed if they tried to escape. Due to these horrendous working and living conditions, as well as the many foreign diseases they caught from the Europeans, the once flourishing Native American population in California greatly diminished. Although it is not known exactly how many people had inhabited the state before the arrival of the Europeans, it is estimated that the Native American population diminished by at least 100,000 people within 50 years of Spanish occupation, if not more.

While the Native Americans declined, the population of the European settlers continued to grow and spread out. In 1781, just a few dozen people, including settlers, soldiers, and their families, settled in what was then known as El Pueblo de Nuestra Señora la

Reina de los Ángeles (The Town of Our Lady the Queen of the Angels), or the Pueblo of Los Ángeles for short. The city of Los Angeles was officially founded on September 4th, 1781, and though it started small, its population grew steadily. By the 1840s, the population had grown to over 1,000 people, and when California joined the United States of America in 1850, it was the largest settlement in California.

Chapter 4 – Mexican California and The Years before California Joined the United States of America (1821–1846)

In the late 18th century, many colonies claimed independence from their monarchy. The United States is one of the more notable and well-known examples, and it declared independence from British rule in 1776. The same feat began taking place with Spain's many colonies in the early 19th century, starting with Ecuador in 1809, which was soon followed by Bolivia and Peru. The next year, Mexico attempted to declare independence, which began the eleven-year Mexican War of Independence. This war ended with the Treaty of Córdoba in 1821, declaring Mexico to be free from Spanish rule.

Even before Mexico officially gained its independence from Spain, California began feeling the consequences. With Spain being rather distracted in its attempts to protect its rule over its many rebelling colonies, the country could not spare as many resources for the settlements in California as before. California, which had previously only traded with Spanish merchants, mostly those located in Mexico, no longer had access to many of their previous clientele. During the Mexican War of Independence, California had essentially lost all of its trading partners, which led local authorities to ease trading restrictions that had previously limited trade to Spanish merchants. California began trading with various countries, including England, Russia, France, and the nearby United States of America. Although California had felt the changes of other Spanish colonies' rebellions for independence, none would cause as big of a ripple as Mexico's.

The Years following Mexico's Independence from Spain

It took many months for the news that California had been acquired by Mexico when the country gained its independence from Spain to actually reach the Spanish settlers in California. Although California would not technically be designated as a territory of Mexico until 1824, the changes were immense and immediate. Before this, all the settled land in California had been owned and controlled by the Franciscan missionaries, but following 1821, Mexico was determined to change that. Mexico allowed Californians to trade with whomever they liked and encouraged international trade. They also, to the Spanish population's surprise, both allowed and encouraged foreign ownership of land to those who were willing to gain citizenship and convert to Catholicism. This was, of course, an immense change for the Californians, who had only ever known the land to be in the control of the Franciscan authority and, therefore, the Spanish Crown. This was only one of the ways the newly founded Republic of Mexico attempted to secularize the state. Many of the large mission ranches were given to civilians, both of Spanish Californian and of Mexican descent, and with the loss of their land, many of the missionaries withdrew. By 1840, essentially all of the remaining mission lands had been parceled out, and the exploitation of the Native Americans had lessened greatly. That being said, although Mexico enforced the end of violence against the Native American population, they did not receive the majority of the divided mission lands. While they did receive some land, their space was limited and far smaller than it had been before the European occupation.

The majority of those who received land were California-born civilians, who became wealthy, following many years where no one could truly be rich but the government officials sent by the Crown and the church. Although a maximum of around 50,000 acres was legally set aside to ensure the land was split fairly, many individuals, who would begin to form an oligarchy of sorts, would receive multiple land grants. Seeing as these properties were so large and the owners were of the elite class of California, most of these territories, known as California ranchos, would employ Native American workers, made up of both the free and mission native population. Some of these ranchos employed hundreds of Native Americans, and it was estimated that by the mid-19th century, around 4,000 Native Americans were working on these properties. Although the Native Americans were technically free, most became what is known as a serf, which is essentially an agricultural peasant-class laborer forced to work for his or her generally rich lord. The Native Americans received shelter, food, and clothing, but very few were paid money or had any potential for upward momentum. The property lords used various deceitful and violent methods to recruit and then maintain their laborers. Seeing as most Californian manufacturing of products stopped when the missions ended, Californians depended on foreign merchants and traders. Since the merchants were generally seeking hides, the Californian landowners usually pushed most of their laborers to focus on raising cattle.

With the Franciscan authority out of the way, California was instead governed by a Mexican-appointed governor. However, although the new system might have sounded good in theory, the politics in California over the subsequent years were shaky and dramatic. Between the years of 1831 and 1836, California had eleven different governors, as well as three men who almost became governor but were rejected by the Californians. Seeing as the Republic of Mexico had little involvement in the actual territory of California, they had little knowledge of who the Californians would accept as a leader and often named candidates they favored, which caused general dissatisfaction amongst the native-born European Californians. Mexico, which was aware of the potential for rebellions, allowed the Californians to reject whomever they wanted, but they could not appoint or vote for their own leadership. In 1836, the population's discontent culminated in a small revolution in which Juan Bautista Alvarado deported the Mexican officials in Monterey after seizing control of the city. Alvarado preached and demanded that California become its own free and sovereign state. Within a few months, Mexico ceded its appointing power and allowed Alvarado to take the governorship in California, which put an end to the discontent for a while.

Although foreign immigration was allowed, it was mostly uncommon throughout the 1820s. However, over the subsequent decades, immigrants, mostly from the United States, began arriving in California. In 1841, John Bidwell and John Bartleson led a group of a couple of hundred people from Missouri to California. This American immigration was encouraged by various Californian elites and the Western Emigration Society, which feared foreign seizure of California. Upon arriving in California, the group was given shelter at one of the Western Emigration Society's ranchos and jobs working for Johann August Sutter, the German-born Swiss businessman who was known to hire settlers from all over to work on his many orchards, vineyards, and wheat fields. As the American population in California began steadily increasing, the country began growing an interest in procuring California as one of its states.

It was during the Mexican California era that the settlers in California began developing their own unique culture separate from that of Spain's. Bull and bear fights became popular pastimes alongside horse racing. All three activities allowed spectators to place bets on their prospective winner. Although the elite, the common people, and the Native American population all lived in the California territory, it was mostly the elite people who had the privilege to enjoy entertaining pastimes. One luxury that elite families indulged in was abnormally long wedding celebrations, which sometimes lasted for over a week. The bride would change dresses many times through the event, and the united elite families would dance and sing for days.

The Lead-Up to the Mexican-American War

However, despite the entertaining events that were attended joyfully by California's elite, dissatisfaction amongst the Californians was growing, as was the United States' interest in the acquisition of California. Although the Mexican-American War would not begin until 1846, in one of the oddest moments in the history of California, the United States accidentally invaded California prematurely. In 1842, Commodore Thomas ap Catesby Jones, who had been the commanding officer of the US Navy's Pacific Squadron, had heard that the United States and Mexico had begun their war. This was likely a rumor that had materialized due to the United States' growing interest in California, but Jones took this as fact and set sail as he had been instructed to do so. Once the war started, he was supposed to seize Monterey, which was the capital of California at the time. Catching just about everyone off guard, Commodore Jones seized the city of Monterey and raised the United States' star-spangled banner as a sign of victory. However, within the day, Jones learned that his intel was nothing but a rumor, forcing the commodore to apologize to the Republic of Mexico and the Californians. He then returned back to the United States.

Chapter 5 – The Mexican-American War and the United States' Acquisition of California (1846–1848)

Before the start of the Mexican-American War, Californian dissatisfaction toward the Republic of Mexico only grew. In 1842, Mexico sent a governor named Pío de Jesús Pico, often shortened to Pío Pico, from Mexico City. Despite being sent by Mexico, Pío Pico had been born at the Mission San Gabriel in California in 1801 and had African, Native American, and European descent. His arrival in California was controversial, to say the least, mostly due to the fact that the last governor of California had actually been Juan Bautista Alvarado, who had pioneered a small rebellion against the Republic of Mexico in order to earn the position. Mexico sending one of its appointed governors was, in many ways, a blow to the Californian sense of pride and independence. Within the next year, dissatisfaction continued to rise, and the concept of an American revolution had begun taking shape. At this time, the population of California consisted of around only 100,000 Native Americans, somewhere between 10,000 and 20,000 settlers of both Spanish or Mexican descent, and less than 3,000 people of foreign descent, of which the largest foreign population was the Americans, whose exact number of inhabitants is unknown.

The Bear Flag Revolt

Although Mexico had instituted many rules upon Americans and other foreigners who attempted to live in California, namely that they had to convert to Catholicism and adopt Mexican citizenship, when Pío Pico took office, he realized enforcing these laws would only lead to a revolution. Pío Pico was essentially left in California by Mexico, which was not helping him or listening to his suggestions or warnings of a potential rebellion. Pico proposed annexing California, which might allow other Western powers to deal with the dissatisfied population instead. However, the government of Mexico would not listen and insisted that they keep California.

Regardless of Mexico's decision not to act in preparation, Pío Pico had been right, and in June of 1846, a small group of Americans living around Sonoma took the city by surprise. They captured the local Mexican colonel, seized the city, and declared independence. To symbolize their freedom, the group raised a handmade flag with a poorly drawn grizzly bear walking toward a red star and the words "California Republic." This is, of course, the origin of the present-day flag of California, which still displays the grizzly bear, red star, and the words "California Republic," although it has gone through many alterations and adjustments over the years. The small group of Americans was led by William B. Ide, who was an American citizen born in Massachusetts, and it slowly moved westward until it finally reached California in late 1845, less than one year before what has come to be known as the Bear Flag Revolt. In the proclamation of the Bear Flag Revolt, William B. Ide called Californians to action by requesting they "assist us in establishing and perpetuating a 'Republican Government' which shall secure to all: civil and religious liberty; which shall detect and punish crime; which shall encourage industry, virtue and literature; which shall leave unshackled by Fetters, Commerce, Agriculture, and Mechanism." Within the month, Captain John Charles Frémont and his troops arrived in Monterey, prepared to defend their newly acquired city against the Republic of Mexico.

The Mexican-American War

It was at this point that Pío Pico's fears became a reality, and he messaged the Republic of Mexico, urging them to send a defense against the invading American troops. However, once again, Pío Pico's requests went mostly unanswered, and Mexico only sent a few hundred soldiers to attempt to defend California. Aware that the Americans would not appreciate his presence, Pío Pico decided to return to Mexico, but before fleeing, he sold his massive acreage off to various Mexican buyers at low prices.

Despite the fact that Frémont and his troops had seized Sonoma, the era of the Republic of California, as the flag proposed, was short lived, as the Mexican-American War had already begun. Technically, Mexico and the United States had actually been in a war before the American seizure of Sonoma. The war broke out following the annexation of Texas, which, like California, was once the property of Mexico. To make matters worse, after acquiring Texas, the United States began making bids to purchase California and New Mexico, which only angered the Republic of Mexico. The United States had plans to respond to Mexico's refusal to negotiate, but before they had the chance, Mexican troops surprised and attacked American troops patrolling the contested area on April 25th, 1846, injuring and killing many. It was technically this event that kickstarted the Mexican-American War, although it took Captain John Charles Frémont's invasion of California for the war over California to truly begin.

In typical American fashion, the country was rather divided on the prospect of war with Mexico. For the most part, southern Democrats favored the war, while many northern Abolitionists were against the war, as they believed that once America acquired the Mexican territories in question, they would become slave states. Regardless of the conflicting American opinions, a war with Mexico had begun, and despite many of the elite Californians being against the movement, California had essentially no say. The United States sent troops south to Mexico and west to inhabit California and New Mexico. Although the elite Californian ranchers sided with Mexico, the settlers and Californian civilians showed no resistance to the occupying American soldiers, and many settlers joined the American troops in the fight against the Republic of Mexico. American General Winfield Scott was sent on a campaign through Mexico under the guidance of President James K. Polk. Although Scott's troops were overall extremely successful in battle, seizing city after city on their campaign and only losing around 1,500 soldiers, the United States lost thousands of soldiers to diseases such as yellow fever, measles, mumps, and smallpox. It is estimated that around 10,000 or more American soldiers died from various illnesses on the Mexican front. Poor sanitation and lack of immunity, which was especially common in soldiers from smaller, rural towns, didn't help the matter either. As the war raged on, the Americans easily took California in January of 1847 when John C. Frémont forced the small number of Mexican and elite Californian soldiers to surrender and sign the Capitulation of Cahuenga. Despite the loss of many soldiers due to illness and the strong Mexican resistance, on September 14th, 1847, after many uninterrupted American victories in both Mexico and California, Winfield Scott and his troops seized Mexico City, which put an end to the actual warfare. However, the conflict was far from over.

The End of the Mexican-American War

After seizing Mexico City, President Polk, his chief clerk, Nicholas Trist, and General Winfield Scott met to negotiate a peace treaty that would put an official end to the war. However, the process was continuously delayed. After months of waiting, on February 2nd, 1848, Nicholas Trist impatiently signed the treaty before both parties were ready, and with that move, the Treaty of Guadalupe Hidalgo was finalized. The treaty detailed that the United States would pay Mexico fifteen million dollars in exchange for both the land and the citizens of New Mexico, Utah, Nevada, Arizona, California, Texas, and western Colorado, which, until then, had all been under Mexican control. Although California had now been acquired by the United States, it would not officially become a state until two years later. Many present-day states took years to become an official American state, as one requirement to achieve statehood was a population of 60,000 people. Seeing as California had less than 10,000 people by the end of the Mexican-American War, it was expected to take many years for it to become an official state. However, what was about to happen later in 1848 would skyrocket the population at an unheard-of speed, allowing California to become a state on September 9th, 1850, in only two years' time.

Chapter 6 – The California Gold Rush (1848–1860)

Johann (John) Sutter

Johann August Sutter was a German-born Swiss who had fled fiscal issues in Switzerland for what was, at the time, the Mexican territory of California. Hoping to make something of himself and rid himself of the financial failures he had endured in Switzerland, Sutter persuaded Mexican officials to accord him some fertile land. He was given territory on the Sacramento River by the Mexican governor, which Sutter named New Switzerland (Nueva Helvetia.) Johann August Sutter became known for hiring and offering lavish shelter to American settlers, and most foreign immigrants were told to find Sutter once they arrived in California since he would help them settle. Although Sutter was in debt when he arrived in California, he spent an excessive amount of money on building Sutter's Fort, creating various businesses, and setting up orchards, vineyards, and wheat fields. Johann changed his name to John and emerged as a typical Californian rancho of the time, and although he was kind and welcoming to American laborers, he, much like the other elite landowners, exploited the Native American laborers.

During the Mexican-American War, soldiers arrived to help the US Army in California. The Capitulation of Cahuenga in January of 1847 ended the Californian theater of the Mexican-American War, which means that not only did Mexico surrender but the American soldiers were also stuck waiting until the war ended in the actual Republic of Mexico. Seeing as the war did not end until the Treaty of Guadalupe Hidalgo was signed by Nicholas Trist almost a year later, on February 2nd, 1848, the American soldiers were in need of jobs to bide their time and make some money. John Sutter had become known as the man Americans should go to when they were in need of work, so hundreds arrived at Sutter's Fort in search of odd jobs. Sutter wanted to build a town, which he would name "Sutterville," for some time, and the arrival of all of the soldiers was the perfect opportunity to do so. Sutter decided his first step would be to build a sawmill, which would not only provide employment for the hordes of men arriving on his property but would also create the lumber needed to construct Sutterville. He began searching for a site.

Finding Gold

Sutter hired James Wilson Marshall, a New Jersey-born carpenter, to find the best location for the sawmill, and during 1847, Marshall chose a location around forty-five miles from Sutter's Fort. He was accompanied by various American laborers to build the sawmill and deepen the American River where the mill would be located. The mill was near completion toward the end of 1847, and on January 24th, 1848, Marshall went to check on the sawmill, seeing as the construction was coming to a close. However, when Marshall went down to the river to check on the sawmill, something shining in a ditch caught his eye. In the words of James Marshall, "I reached my hand down and picked it up; it made my heart thump, for I was certain it was gold...Then I saw another." Only nine days before the signing of the Treaty of Guadalupe Hidalgo, which put an end to the Mexican-American War, James Marshall found multiple gold nuggets in the American River, which would drastically change the course of California's history.

The Gold Rush

Seeing as the gold Marshall discovered was on Sutter's property, he quickly relayed the information to his employer, and the two men decided to become partners. Although they tried to keep the fortune a secret, the news leaked. It is hard to know if this was due to the other men who had been working on the sawmill or some other source, but before long, prospective gold miners arrived from all over. Within six months, the hills near the river were covered in tents and wooden huts, which housed over 4,000 men who were prepared to mine for their fortune. The first news of Sutter's fortune reached Asia and then Central and South America. Hundreds of men sailed thousands of miles from China and hiked across Panama, often risking death due to illnesses they'd pick up on the trip as a result of poor sanitation, nutrition, and contact with other populations. While the travelers did suffer, the illnesses killed far more of the Native Americans who came into contact with the prospective gold miners than the gold miners themselves. However, within those first months, the majority of the tents were not of foreigners but of local Californians, which included Hispanic Californians, Sutter's laborers, and Native Americans. Over the course of the next month, some other groups arrived from nearby states and territories such as Utah, Oregon, Hawaii, Mexico, China, and Chile.

The Forty-Niners

Despite news having reached the southern countries in the Americas, it took nearly a year for the news to reach and set in as fact in the United States. Seeing as there was no railroad or easy way to access California as of yet, the news would not reach the eastern United States until boats sailed the Atlantic Ocean on their way for California. Once the news had reached the United States, no one was sure if it was true, and seeing as it was no easy task to reach California, which by boat would take over half a year, sailing the dangerous waters through the Isthmus of Panama or "around the Horn," citizens were not willing to take a chance on a rumor. By mid-1848, William Tecumseh Sherman, an American army officer, was eager to know if the rumor was true, both for his own curiosity and for his fellow Americans who had no idea of the validity of the rumor. Sherman asked one of his officers, Colonel Richard Barnes Mason, who was California's military governor at the time, if he would go to Sutter's property and see for himself if the rumor was true. Of course, he discovered that there was, in fact, gold to be found. Mason reported the news to President Polk, who proceeded to make an official declaration on December 5th, 1848, sparking a new dream in the American citizens.

That official announcement of gold in California changed California's future in an instant, and by the next day, almost anyone who was left in the territory of California had set up a campsite on the hills near the gold-laden river. However, no one could have expected the insane number of people who arrived over the course of the following year. The immigrants, known as the "forty-niners," arrived in California by the thousands throughout 1849. Tens of thousands of people arrived at San Francisco's port after traveling for miles on the rough oceans, and a few thousand wagons came from all over America, carrying around 40,000 people, despite the hazardous, long, bumpy ride. It is estimated around 80,000 forty-niners arrived over the course of the year, and over 250,000 total had immigrated to California by 1853. They all had one common goal: to hopefully strike gold. Seeing as there was so much competition, only a lucky few actually struck gold, and since the locals knew they could take advantage of the newcomers, the cost of living and food was high. Those who were tired of digging or had some starter money opened businesses, stores, and/or became farmers, which helped develop California's local economy. Before the Gold Rush, its economy was practically non-existent. Despite the hard, strenuous work and long hours, the gold miners rarely got a full night's sleep, seeing as they lived in overpopulated areas and typically slept in primitive shelters, such as tents and huts. However, seeing as two billion dollars in gold was extracted from the river and surrounding areas, many did strike gold, and they would generally invest in hiring miners to continue looking for them until they could replace the laborers with machines.

California Becoming a State

Although there are many different requirements set in place for a territory to become an official state in the United States of America, in 1848, when America officially acquired California, the main thing in California's way was the population requirement. At the time, California needed to have 60,000 people for it to officially achieve statehood, and when it was won by the United States as a result of the Mexican-American War, California only had a measly 7,000 people or so. Many states took years until they had a large enough population to gain statehood, and since California's population was so small, it seemed like it could take at least a decade for enough Americans to emigrate to California. However, all of that changed with Sutter and Marshall's discovery of gold in January of 1848 in present-day Sacramento. In 1849, far more than 60,000 people arrived, meaning that California blew past the required population number to join the Union and become an official state. Although there were many debates, on September 9th, 1850, California was officially recognized as a state by Congress. This decision was sped up not only by the discovery of gold but also by the fact that rancheros and local commanders were impatiently waiting on reforms that could best be decided by a central government. They decided to draw up their own constitution modeled after those of other states. The constitution declared California as a free-labor state, meaning that it was anti-slavery and that laborers were independent of their employers and could technically work their way to riches. As an interesting side note, California was never a designated territory of the United States, unlike other states out west, such as Oregon.

After 1850

In the years prior to California achieving statehood, laws were created and upheld by local miners and townspeople, who, without any official government, were forced to handle local affairs themselves. However, even after September 9th, 1850, when California joined the United States, no central government truly took control of the state, and local officers did not want to act without instruction, which frustrated the local civilians. By 1851, the dissatisfied people in San Francisco formed a law-and-order group called the "Vigilance Committee," which inspired other mining towns and Californian cities to do the same. Although this worked for a short period, by the end of the year, most of the groups had disbanded, and local authorities took control.

By the end of the Gold Rush, more than 300,000 people had permanently emigrated to California. In many of the Gold Rush towns, there were businesses and economies set up around the mines, but in others, there was nothing but a ghost town, as once the gold supply had dried up, the miners would pack up and leave. In the years following 1852, the Gold Rush slowed down, especially as technologies improved. Beforehand, the panning method was the most common way to find gold. This method involved an individual miner swirling water in a strainer. However, with time came the wooden "rocker" and other creations that changed the face of mining. The majority of these mining inventions were more efficient, as they allowed many laborers to work together rather than just one individual man working on his own. As a result, the richer miners formed companies. Soon enough, the gold in the rivers was all excavated, and the miners moved to the nearby rocks, where they mined shafts with pickaxes dozens of feet in the ground. Underground tunnels began stretching across many miles, and men working in teams for large businesses spent their days below ground, searching for gold. Although many of the miners who had hoped to strike it rich on their own had left after the 1850s, over the next few decades, the gold hunt still existed, and it was dominated by large joint-stock companies rather than individual men.

The Effects of the Gold Rush

It is without a doubt that the effects of the Gold Rush dramatically changed the territory of California. Although not many individuals became rich from the rush itself, plenty of businessmen and shop owners profited greatly off of the booming population and the need for entertainment, food, shelter, and other resources. Settlers from all over the globe arrived in California, which had previously only been made up of Native Americans, Spanish Californians, and Mexicans. The Gold Rush caused the population to grow almost twenty times as large in less than a decade, and it is the reason California was admitted as a state so quickly. With the new influx of people, California was forced to build up its cities, and a local economy developed. California would quickly become the biggest powerhouse in western America, both economically and politically. Immigrants benefited from California's vast expanse of available land, many fishable waterways, ideal farming climate, and fertile soil.

Chapter 7 – California during the Civil War and in the First Few Years of Development (1860–1869)

Initial Societal Issues

By the beginning of the 1860s, the population of California had well surpassed 300,000 residents, and seeing as the census did not usually take into account the many spread-out native tribes around the state, there was likely more than 300,000. Since the start of the Gold Rush, the population had tripled, but by 1860, gold mining was no longer the main resource attracting immigrants. California had mild temperatures, exceptionally long growing seasons, and fertile soil. All types of farming flourished over the decades following the Gold Rush, but cattle ranching was likely the most profitable in the 1860s. The farmers and manufacturers who arrived alongside the gold miners were much needed in the newly founded state, which had been relying on foreign merchants for most manufactured items since the expulsion of the Franciscan missionaries by the Republic of Mexico. However, despite the fact that California's internal production was increasing and its own local market was growing, farmers, manufacturers, producers, and businessmen were all very aware of the losses they experienced due to the lack of a link to the rest of the United States. Unlike many of the cities elsewhere in the United States, which had boomed gradually as railways were built and cities expanded, the California Gold Rush pushed California's population to grow far faster than cities usually do, which meant the state's cities were not quite prepared for the needs of a large permanent society.

The lack of a railway was not the only way California's cities were not prepared for large permanent settlements. Toward the mid-19th century, many issues arose between different ethnic groups who had arrived in California for the same purpose, to make a fortune or at least some money for themselves and their family. Although American citizens who had arrived from the eastern states generally seemed to get along with European immigrants, whether they spoke the English tongue or not, they generally resented non-English-speaking and non-European miners and civilians. Prejudice and racial issues began arising between the American miners and the Latin and Chinese miners. Over time, the mining population migrated away from the Gold Rush rivers and mines and to the newly established cities. Many of the Chinese miners congregated in San Francisco, where they settled and opened businesses, establishing the United States of America's very first Chinatown. The Chinese who continued to search for gold continued to feel harsh treatment from their American peers, who had developed a racist anti-Chinese mindset. This meant that California not only became a difficult place for the diverse foreigners who had arrived throughout the 19th century but also for the Americans, especially those from the Confederate States, who were not used to foreigners and had little respect or understanding of the diversity of California.

California's Relationship with Slavery

Another massive societal issue the newly founded Californian cities were forced to deal with was the varying opinion on slavery. Although the Californian constitution had technically ordained California as a free-labor state, the agreement was not exactly specific, and there were many easy ways to find loopholes in the text. It was not only the Californians who were unsure about their stance on slavery but also the other states, which often fought about how strict California's slavery stance should be. This debate is part of the reason why California was not admitted as a state in 1849, even though it had met the population requirement. During the Gold Rush, businessmen and mining companies from the Confederate States sent hundreds if not thousands of African slaves to mine for gold. Though California was determined as a free-labor, anti-slave state, one way these slave owners got around the rules was by not officially declaring the slaves as citizens. Instead, they were workers and were designated as citizens for states that allowed slavery. Thus, while slavery was occurring on Californian soil, the rules were vague enough that there were rarely consequences. By 1860, there were a few thousand African Americans living in California, the majority of them living freely in San Francisco, Sacramento, and other smaller mining towns in the north, where slavery was commonly rejected and the population was less prejudiced.

Overall, the issue of slavery was not settled in California as it may have seemed to have been when the country formed its constitution. The state was essentially separated into those known as Free Soilers in the north, who believed California should be a free state, and those who were self-titled the Chivs (shortened from chivalry) in the south, who wanted California to be a slave state. This split was no different than what many of the southern states had been seeing. Something similar occurred in the state of Virginia, which ended up splitting into the anti-slavery state of West Virginia and pro-slavery Virginia. Although the state of California was never technically separated, nor was it the common opinion that separation should occur, the difference of opinions toward slavery only caused more societal issues for the newly forming cities and growing population in California.

California's Role in the Civil War

Although the state of California had been and is still to this day overwhelmingly Democratic-leaning, at the time of the 1860 presidential election, Republican candidate Abraham Lincoln won the majority in California, albeit only by a small margin. There are a number of reasons as to why California suddenly voted Republican, one being that the businessmen who held a lot of power and property in California were mostly Republican. The other reason is likely that the state was not, for the most part, pro-slavery, which was a key part of the Democratic Party's campaign. However, despite the fact that Lincoln won in California, the votes were closer than in almost any other state, as the other states generally had a sweeping majority vote during the 1860 presidential election. The differences of opinion on slavery were, of course, not only an issue in California, and by 1861, just after Lincoln's inauguration, the American Civil War broke out between the Union (anti-slavery) and the Confederate (pro-slavery) states. Despite the fact that there were still many powerful Californian southerners who believed slavery was their right, during the Civil War, California supported the anti-slavery Union armies. This led some of the dissatisfied Californian southerners to create pro-Confederate groups, such as the well-known Los Angeles Mounted Rifles and the Knights of the Golden Circle.

California would be a great help to the Union military by providing both soldiers and financing. Although California was far away from most of the fighting, many believe that it was, in fact, California's gold mines that helped sway the course of the war in favor of the Union. The state of California was rather remote when the Civil War broke out, but the state still supplied the Union military with thousands of soldiers. They mainly helped fight in nearby states, such as Arizona and New Mexico. After the initial attack on Fort Sumter, which is what began the Civil War, many anti-slavery Californians were inspired to join the military, and by the end of the war, over 17,000 Californians enlisted. Despite the state's distance from most of the fighting, California would actually have the highest Union military joining per capita ratio in all of America, which was partly because the population of California was still quite small at the start of the Civil War. Those who could not join the military also held pro-Union rallies, most notably in San Francisco, which would help inspire many men to join the movement over the course of the war.

Despite the large number of Californian soldiers who ended up supporting the Union military, California's largest contribution to the war was not in manpower but in financial and material contributions. California was one of the largest funders of the United States Sanitary Commission, a Union medical organization. To help fund the Union organizations, military, and government, California sent shipments of gold out to the Union forces in any way possible. Seeing as there were still no railways at the time of the outbreak of the American Civil War, the safest way to get gold to the Union was by ship, which mostly sailed from the San Francisco Bay. The United States government began sending Union military troops to San Francisco in order to protect the gold shipments, which sometimes amounted to over a million dollars. Typically, lesser amounts would be shipped out, but all these shipments were constantly threatened by Confederate raiders on steamships.

Building the Railway

After many years of isolation, the necessity for a railroad connecting the rest of the United States of American to California increased. It seemed as if the construction of a railway could no longer wait, and in 1862, Abraham Lincoln signed the Pacific Railway Act. Although California had become an official state in 1850, construction had been delayed due to many debates over whether the railways should be built through the North or the South of the United States. Of course, when President Lincoln signed the Pacific Railway

Chapter 8 – California Post Civil War until the End of the 19th Century (1865–1900)

The Expansion of the Railroads and the Impact on California's Cities

Although there had already been some short local railroads built in and around California during the Gold Rush, there were no railroads connecting the state to far-off destinations, but the lack of railroads didn't stop people from arriving during the 1840s and 1850s. However, the transcontinental railroad, which was built by the Central Pacific and Union Pacific Railroads and completed on May 10th, 1869, would drastically change California's immigration patterns. The western terminus had been constructed in Sacramento, although the ultimate goal was to have the transcontinental railway reach the booming city of San Francisco. Originally, train passengers would get off the train in Sacramento and then embark on paddle steamers that would take them to nearby cities, including San Francisco. However, on September 6th, 1869, the Western Pacific Railroad completed the railway that would connect Sacramento and the San Francisco Bay so that routes could end at the Alameda Terminal, only ten miles or so by boat to San Francisco. A few months later, the terminus was moved a few miles north to Oakland, which would facilitate the connection of the transcontinental line to the rest of California's cities. Initially, the arrival of the transcontinental railroad had the effect California had expected: the northern cities that the train line reached expanded their economies and population as drastically as during the Gold Rush. However, what the northern businessmen, who had pushed for the railway, had not expected was the expansion in the south of California over the next few decades, which would take power and business away from the previously booming north.

When the transcontinental railroad reached the north of California, passengers moving to settle and farm would quickly discover that almost all of the area within one hundred miles or more of the terminus was already owned by big businesses, which were hoping to capitalize off the passengers, and by large ranchos that had been kept in the family since the time of Mexico's ownership of California. Although many easterners settled in the ever-expanding city of San Francisco, those looking to farm and own some property quickly began to spread southward in search of vacant land. By the 1880s, the state of California had lowered the ticket costs to promote travel and expanded the railroad hundreds of miles southward. In 1885, the railroad finally reached Los Angeles, which had a population of just over 10,000 people at the time. Within the next decade, the population of Los Angeles and Southern California grew by tens of thousands, and by the turn of the century, there would be over 100,000 people in Los Angeles alone.

As the railroads expanded, companies bought up all of the land surrounding the terminuses with the intention of constructing buildings that suited every type of buyer and traveler who was arriving. Throughout the end of the 19th century, California became littered with resort hotels, official state parks, and other gimmicks to bring in tourists who would hopefully settle and help grow California's economy.

California's Tourism Scene

Just about every American, even those with no intention of settling in California, were interested in visiting the state. Between their fascination with the Gold Rush and the promotions from the railroads and businessmen of California advertising unique landscapes of the state, California quickly became a popular tourist spot and a dream destination for many eastern Americans. In 1865, even Abraham Lincoln was quoted to have said, "I have long desired to see California; the production of her gold mines has been a marvel to me...I have it now in purpose when the railroad is finished, to visit your wonderful state." Although many of the temporary travelers arriving on the trains to California had the intention of striking it rich mining for gold, which by the time of the train lines had become something of a fool's errand, others arrived just to see the Gold Rush in action after hearing rumors of the frenzy for years. As the train line expanded, the gold mines were no longer the only destinations advertised to travelers. Tourists began seeking out California's unique landscape, the Pacific coastline, redwood forests, and the cliffs and waterfalls of the Yosemite Valley. The railroads and big California companies and businesses quickly realized it was becoming more profitable to set up businesses near attractions for tourists than for Californian locals, so hotels, themed restaurants, and pre-packaged tours became more and more common.

California's Conservationism Movements

As big businesses and the railroad companies began profiting off of California's tourism by setting up hotels, railways, and stores, more and more of California's land was being eaten up by tourist attractions. Although many tourists were happy to get on the train, stay in the gimmicky hotels, go on some tours of California's unique landscapes, and then head back home, other tourists were noticing how the landscapes were actually being transformed and destroyed by the tourism. It was California's jaw-dropping glacial Yosemite Valley that inspired Scottish-born John Muir to find a way to protect the state's incredible flora and fauna. John Muir arrived in California just after the transcontinental train line was completed, and after spending some years working and traveling in California, he noticed how the state that he had fallen in love with was changing around him. Muir began connecting with other nature lovers in the Sierra Club, and together, the group founded a conservation movement whose main goal was to protect the natural wonders of California. The conservation group, as well as others inspired by Muir and his fellow Californian nature lovers, began getting in contact with the state and national governments in order to put some rules in place that would preserve as much nature as possible. Although the group would have many small successes during the 1870s and 1880s, in 1890, they achieved Muir's original goal of protecting the Yosemite Valley with the creation of Yosemite National Park.

California's Native American Population during the Late 19th Century

John Muir and the other conservationists were not the only ones attempting to protect California's nature and landscape against the big businesses and railroad ventures. While the boom in population benefited many of the American Californians who had set up businesses during the Gold Rush, it caused mass destruction to the population who had been living there previously. The Native Americans of California had suffered with every new immigration pattern that had arrived in the state, with the expansion of the railroads perhaps one of the worst things to happen to the native population to date. As the Americans arrived in hordes on the trains, planning to settle in the lands in the south and east that had not been bought and developed by businesses, the Native American territory continued to get smaller and smaller. History repeated itself when the native population, which had reestablished their migratory ways of living over the previous decades, were forced into communities on small restricted preserved lands known as reservations, similar to when California was under Franciscan authority. The native tribes, which had just found freedom from the ranchos and managed to find space during the Gold Rush to live their migratory lifestyles away from the coast where the Americans had settled, were once again being shoved out of their own territories. With every given year, the railroads expanded their tracks, bringing along Americans and Europeans who gradually settled on more and more of the previously occupied native land. As more settlers arrived, the Native American reservation lands became more and more unfavorable, as the fertile territories were given to prospective white American farmers. The Native Americans were forced to get used to the pattern. The railroads expanded, they were moved to a smaller territory, settlers found something of interest while exploring nearby territories, and the native tribes were once again moved, their territory gradually being reduced and migration becoming no longer possible.

Of course, the Native American population was not just amicably allowing the settlers to take their land, and many tribes, which were small to begin with, were almost completely wiped out trying to stick up for their land. Even the Native American success stories were rarely positive, seeing as victories only lasted until the next settlers arrived. One of the most well-known examples of the far from harmonious Native American and white American relations was in the Modoc War, which lasted from 1872 to 1873. Before the 1860s, the Modoc population lived peacefully in the Tule Lake region in northeast California. However, in 1864, after many years of living remotely, virtually in isolation, Americans who had arrived for the Gold Rush wanted to settle and mine in the Modoc tribe's territory. The United States created a reservation for them to move to in Klamath, Oregon, around forty miles away from their previous territory in Tule Lake, California. Aware of the potential for war and knowing that the Americans would be more prepared than them, the Modoc population moved as peacefully as possible to the granted reservation land in southern Oregon. Although the Modoc population resentfully resituated themselves in their new territory, they planned to find a way to return to their home. Finally, in 1870, around 175 of the Modoc who had been moved to the Klamath reservation returned to Tule Lake under the leadership of Kientpoos (known as Captain Jack). The group remained there for almost two years until US Army commanders were instructed to, if possible, peacefully return the Modoc to their reservation. Of course, the angered Native Americans were not willing to peacefully return to the government reservation, and by 1873, the US Army's orders changed, and they were instructed to use more force to remove the Modoc people from their homeland. Thus began the Modoc War.

On January 17th, 1873, 400 armed men from the United States Army, most of whom were on horseback, surprised and attacked the 50 or so Modoc who were defending Tule Lake. Although the Modoc population was caught off guard, they knew the unique landscape of lava beds and cliffs well, and they used it to their advantage. Despite the fact that the Americans had advanced Civil War weaponry in comparison to the Native Americans' slow, out-of-date muzzle-loading weapons, the Modoc managed to kill a few dozen American soldiers and forced the rest to retreat. Following that brief violent interaction, the Modoc's leader Kientpoos (Captain Jack), accompanied by other Modoc, met with General Edward Canby to discuss peaceful solutions. The period of peace and discussion lasted a few months, but within time, the Modoc stopped arriving at scheduled meetings, and both sides became aggravated. On April 11th, 1873, the two sides had planned to have a peaceful discussion, but both the US soldiers and the Modoc people showed up armed. At the April 11th meeting, Kientpoos (Captain Jack), who was determined to find a solution, requested a promise from General Canby that the Modoc tribe could have a place in their homeland, which Canby could not promise. This was the straw that broke the camel's back, and the Modoc tribe attacked and killed General Canby. Canby was the only US Army general to die in the overarching American Indian Wars, so it is safe to say that after his death on April 11th, the United States Army was beyond peaceful agreements. On April 15th, the United States Army sent 600 soldiers to attack the Modoc, and after only a few days of fighting, they forced the Modoc people to split up and flee eastward. Of course, the United States soldiers were not going to allow the Modoc tribe to get away after killing their general, and over the course of the next month, the Modoc groups were pursued. Within time, one of the small Modoc groups that had split off from the main assembly was captured, and it agreed to help the United States Army track down the rest of the Modoc and, more specifically, their leader Kientpoos (Captain Jack). The rest of the Modoc were captured on June 1st, and while most were sent to various Oklahoma reservations, four months later, Captain Jack and six other Modoc were hung on account of murder. It would be thirty-six years before the Modoc that had been sent to the reservations in Oklahoma were allowed to return to their families on the Klamath reservations. The Modoc people lost their homeland, and by losing their home, they also lost their lifestyle, diet, artistry, traditions, and other ways of life that were unique to their location. Although the Modoc tribe put up a good fight, they had little chance against the United States Army, which had not only far more people and more advanced weapons but also money. In just the Modoc War alone, the United States Army spent 500,000 dollars.

The Modoc were far from the only tribe to be pushed out of their ancestral home by the settlers and United States Army. Throughout what is known as the American Indian Wars, hundreds of tribes were forced onto reservations, and thousands of Native Americans lost their life. While this was occurring all over the United States, the previously diverse and peaceful Californian tribes were hit especially hard, and by 1900, there was only estimated to be about 15,000 Native American people left in California. Although the main reason for the Native American population decreasing from over a hundred thousand to only 15,000 was displacements to other states, thousands of Native Americans died due to war or illnesses brought by tourists and settlers.

Mexican Californians and California Ranchos during the Late 19th Century

Although not as destructive as it was to the Native American population, the arrival of the new American settlers over the course of the 19th century was not entirely positive for the other Californians who had thrived in the territory before the Gold Rush. While the elite Mexicans in California still did quite well during the 1850s, many white American miners developed prejudices toward Mexican and Hispanic miners during the Gold Rush. Over the years, this prejudice reached even the richest of California's Mexicans. As American settlers arrived, hoping to purchase land in California, many were disappointed to find out that much of the land along the Pacific coast and near the expanding cities had been granted to Mexican and Spanish civilians after the expulsion of the Franciscan missionaries. Discussion of whether these land grants should still be valid, seeing as the territory had not been bought and now belonged to the United States, became commonplace. Mexican and Spanish landowners were forced to spend thousands of dollars in court disputing their case, which, even if they won, often drained them of the money needed to upkeep the property. Over the course of the decades following the Gold Rush, the white American population began gradually outnumbering the Mexican population, and within time, the Mexicans and Hispanics lost most of their power in the state of California. By the 1880s, the Spanish and Mexican population would become a small minority of the population, and they would be mostly forgotten by the growing white American population. It would not be until the 20th century, when Spanish and Mexican immigration recommenced, that the Spanish and Mexican population began to be able to have more of a say in California's politics and lifestyle once again.

Feminism in California

Although equality of the genders was nowhere near present-day standards, overall, California was more progressive than other American states in the mid-19th century. Of course, women were still not able to vote, and the "progressive" rights were only accorded to white women in California. However, white wives were technically able to own property in 1850, which was not common in southern states. Although California would not allow women to vote until 1911, in 1884, a Californian feminist politician, Marietta L. Stow, became the first female to run for vice president of the United States. While Marietta L. Stow was faced with inequality herself, her tagline while running for the governor of California was "anti-monopoly, anti-ring, and anti-Chinese." This was common, as the various groups of minorities (and those who faced inequality) in California were no less prejudiced against each other than the white Americans.

Chinese Population in California toward the End of the 19th Century

If Marietta L. Stow's political 1880s campaign, "anti-monopoly, anti-ring, and anti-Chinese," was of any indication, throughout the 19th century, the prejudice against the Chinese immigrants only worsened. During the Gold Rush, tens of thousands of Chinese immigrants arrived alongside foreigners from the United States, Europe, and South America, and discrimination against the Chinese in the mining camps began almost immediately. By the 1860s and 1870s, as gold mining transitioned into being owned by big corporations instead of individual miners, the majority of the Chinese immigrants who had arrived for the Gold Rush had moved to rural areas. Although most of California's population by the turn of the century had arrived on train tracks laid by Chinese immigrants who had been living in California during the Gold Rush, when the national economy worsened in the 1870s, many Americans felt that it was unfair for the Chinese laborers to be hired while there were "Americans" without work. Technically, it was true that Chinese laborers had been given many jobs, jobs that may have gone to "Americans," but this was mainly due to the fact that there were no regulations against paying the minorities less than white Americans working the same job. The Chinese were being taken advantage of by bosses who would not have hired white Americans to work the job in the first place since it would cost them more. The reputation of the Chinese was not helped by the fact that Chinese immigrants continued to arrive over the course of the 1870s, which made Americans discriminate more against Chinese Americans, some of who had lived in California for two decades or more, as they felt their work was even more threatened than before. In 1880, the United States would begin to regulate Chinese immigration, and in 1882, the United States signed the Chinese Exclusion Act, which put an end to Chinese immigration altogether until 1890.

Although the majority of the Chinese immigrants who arrived to mine gold in the 1850s immediately went to work on farms in rural areas after the Gold Rush came to an end, 24 percent of the Chinese population in California moved to San Francisco. San Francisco had become a safe place or at least the safest place for Chinese immigrants in the state of California. As the city's Chinatown grew, Chinese Americans could expect to find restaurants with the food they grew up with, work under people who spoke their language, and fellow Chinese speakers to become friends with. As anti-Chinese sentiment grew and was openly displayed in rallies and protests, the Chinese population was thriving in San Francisco (at least in comparison to other states and areas in California), and before long, many of the Chinese immigrants who had been working in the rural areas moved to the cities. By the turn of the century, more than half of California's Chinese population had moved to urban areas, 45 percent of which were actually living in and around San Francisco.

The majority of the Chinese immigrants in California were men since most immigrants had the intention of striking it rich during the California Gold Rush and returning home to their families or bringing their families to California. The Chinese women in California had it quite a bit worse than the men. The workforce for women in California was already limited, and on top of the anti-Chinese prejudice, women had an almost impossible time finding work. Those who managed to make it to California were often tricked into becoming essentially slaves of the sex trade, and in 1870, over 60 percent of Chinese women in California were prostitutes, with no way to get out of the unfair contracts.

California Heading into the New Century

If California's history in the mid-19th century is defined by the Gold Rush and its many effects, California between the end of the Civil War until the turn of the century can almost entirely be defined by the completion of the railway. Regardless of the often-disastrous effects on the Chinese, Mexican, Spanish, and Native American populations, California was expanding at record rates. By the 1890s, California had already had its first real estate boom and real estate collapse; tourism was being established, with buildings to accommodate tourists being built so quickly that conservatism was founded; and the Native American population had been reduced to merely 5 percent of what it had been before the Gold Rush. With almost all of the state's gold being excavated, California began developing its own unique diversified economy with mining of other minerals, as well as farming that had not yet been accessible to America. However, by 1900, California was no longer the only state in the West, as the entire Pacific coast had been established by newly formed American states. Overall, despite the inequality amongst the races, over the course of the 19th century and still in the present day, California became a desirable location for most immigrants coming to the United States hoping to achieve the "American Dream."

Chapter 9 – California in the 20th Century (1900–2000)

Unlike most states and cities, which received more organized immigration and gradual economic growth, California's Gold Rush created a population boom that the state was not yet prepared for. The cities were small and unfit for the influx of people, and the local economy was unestablished, but by the beginning of the 20th century, the peak of the Gold Rush had ended over half a century ago. In 1850, the population of California was 92,597, and by 1900, the population had grown to 1,485,053 people, many of whom had arrived far after the Gold Rush had ended. By the turn of the century, the over a million people who now inhabited California had established ways to build the local Californian economy, with one of the primary ways being oil production. In 1855, oil was discovered less than forty miles away from the still small Los Angeles in Pico Canyon, and in 1865, another oil well was unearthed in Humboldt County of Northern California. When the oil was discovered, America did not have much of a need for it, but over the course of the 19th and 20th centuries, the demand for oil would skyrocket, as automobiles became commonplace. By the year 1900, California was one of the leading oil-producing states in the United States, which would help establish California's economy and workforce and give immigrants another reason to choose California to settle in.

San Francisco Earthquake

Despite the fact that California's economy and the population were growing at record speeds with every passing year, the cities were oftentimes ill-equipped for the incoming settlers, and, in turn, the settlers were ill-equipped for California's unique topography, climate, and natural occurrences. No different than the present day, the state of California was no stranger to forest fires, floods, and earthquakes, and while all of which could be destructive, the Native American communities who had lived in the territory before had adopted strategies to cope with the potential natural disasters. The American settlers, on the other hand, were, for the most part, used to eastern climates and nature, which, in comparison to California, is much more stable. They were not prepared for the potential natural disasters. As buildings went up, few had been constructed with natural disasters in mind, which is why the San Francisco earthquake of 1906 hit California so hard.

Although San Francisco and the state of California had experienced other earthquakes, namely two only a few years beforehand in 1898 and 1900, on the morning of April 18th, 1906, San Francisco and the state of California was hit with an earthquake the likes the settlers had never experienced before. Before sunrise, the city of San Francisco was hit with a 7.7 to 7.9 magnitude earthquake, which was described to have sounded "like the roar of 10,000 lions." At five in the morning, the entire city shook, and seeing as the city was not prepared, glass roofs shattered all over the streets, City Hall crumbled, and many massive uncontrollable fires spread around the city. Although the earthquake of 1906 was beyond damaging, it would be the fire that caused the most destruction in the city. The fire, which raged on for three more days, destroyed close to 30,000 buildings on around 500 blocks in the, at this point, newly constructed San Francisco. Seeing as firemen of the early 20th century were still ill-equipped for fighting fires and those in California were almost completely inexperienced in fighting massive fires, the fire department was unable to put out the fire, and it would not be until the rain fell on April 21ˢᵗ that the fire would be put out once and for all. In less than a week, the city was destroyed; it is estimated around 350 million dollars' worth of property was lost and that around 4,000 people died due to the earthquake and resulting fires.

The earthquake, which lasted for only a minute, would cause effects that would ripple throughout the entire state of California. Due to San Francisco's response to the event, it became quickly obvious how common class, race, and political issues were in the state of California. Following the 1906 earthquake and fires, a quarter of a million people were left homeless, driving a wedge even further between the elite upper-class citizens and the working class who had suffered the greatest. Seeing as the city of San Francisco needed to be rebuilt, relief money quickly came flooding in from the United States, whose president at the time was Theodore Roosevelt, as well as from European and Asian countries that had become well-acquainted trade partners with the state of California. The rebuilding of the city was put into the hands of the mayor, James Phelan, and his formed committee of the city's rich businessmen, who quickly set up cramped, poorly taken care of refugee camps for San Francisco's homeless.

Although inequalities between the working class and the elite have technically existed in California since the very beginning of its history, it became more obvious by how the committee responded to the 1906 crises in San Francisco. Although 250,000 people had lost their homes to the fires and earthquake, rather than focusing on rebuilding homes, the committee set up refugee camps and focused on rebuilding businesses. Those who had been poor before 1906 suffered the worst since the poorer communities often lived and worked in the same buildings, which meant that if someone lost their workplace to the fire or earthquake, they lost their home as well. The various racial minorities in San Francisco, who already had it hard enough, suffered greatly from the events of 1906. Almost all of San Francisco's Chinatown burnt down in the fires, which many directly associate to the committee's attempts to protect the Nob Hill neighborhood, where many of the wealthy city leaders resided, as they used dynamite on Chinatown buildings to slow down the spread of the fire. However, this action not only destroyed Chinese homes and businesses but also fueled the flames. After the rain put out the fire, soldiers, who were instructed to protect and guard the city, turned a blind eye and allowed men, women, and fellow soldiers to loot Chinatown of anything that had survived the fire, meaning the Chinese lost everything they owned of value, even what didn't burn. Lootings became commonplace occurrences in the aftermath of the earthquake and fires, and the ill-equipped police force was instructed to shoot looters. However, they would often disproportionately shoot racial minorities, although almost all of the poor civilians were looting at the time. San Francisco was gradually rebuilt with fires, earthquakes, and other natural disasters in mind to avoid any other crises such as what occurred in 1906, and as the other cities in California were built, city planners learned from San Francisco and planned ahead.

Expansion of the South of California

Following the events of the San Francisco earthquake and fires of 1906, San Francisco and, by proxy, Northern California became less desirable for new settlers. Although California's population would increase by 60 percent by 1910, the majority of the population was no longer heading for the San Francisco Bay Area but the ever-expanding south of California. In 1900, San Francisco represented almost a quarter of California's population, with around 342,782 people living there, but by 1910, the population had grown by less than 100,000 people even though California's overall population had grown by close to a million.

The south of California, which was now easily accessible from the train lines, was rumored to have incredible growing conditions, and it was growing at record speeds, with most of the growth centered specifically around Los Angeles, which had the advantage of nearby oil wells. At the turn of the century, Los Angeles's population was just barely over 100,000, but within a decade, the population had grown to 319,198, and by 1920, the population of Los Angeles would have tens of thousands of more people than San Francisco. Part of this rise in population was due to the influx of Mexican immigrants who arrived over the course of the 1910s as the country dealt with its bloody years of revolution. The other reason for the growth in population was the creation of the film industry, which boomed at the beginning of the 20th century, bringing hordes of prospective movie stars to Hollywood. They were no different than the forty-niners of Gold Rush, as they too had dreams of becoming rich.

The Film Industry

In many foreigners' eyes, California is now synonymous with Hollywood and its film industry. Hollywood's first film, *The Count of Monte Cristo*, was completed in 1908, but Hollywood's film industry would not truly begin to pick up steam until the 1910s. Until the 20th century, all American films had been produced on the East Coast, but in 1908, when Thomas Edison founded the Motion Picture Patents Company, which essentially wiped out the United States' film industry companies with costly lawsuits, the film companies began moving as far away from Edison as possible. In 1910, the first film was shot entirely in California, and by 1911, California's first movie studio opened on Hollywood's Sunset Boulevard. California became the perfect location for filmmakers. It had predictable weather, optimal sunlight, every type of background landscape, and, best of all, the filmmakers could not be sued by the Motion Picture Patents Company. As movie production increased in California, featuring beautiful idyllic shots of nature, the state essentially received free advertising, and hordes of settlers arrived, both to be in the movies and to visit the settings the movies depicted.

World War I

Although California and the other western states were far less involved in World War I, as well as other wars, than the eastern American states, the state of California still played its part during the Great War, which lasted from 1914 to 1918. Throughout World War I, California's greatest contribution was to the Allies' aviation sector of the military. During World War I, nearly 200,000 employees worked in the aircraft industry in California, and by the end of the war, just the southern region of the state alone would contribute around 17,000 aircraft to the United States military efforts. Seeing as the aircraft industry was growing rapidly in California, pilot training became commonplace, and the state sent over ten thousand pilots to aid the Allies in World War I. Thanks to the aircraft needs of the United States military during World War I, California's economy flourished in the 1910s. Hundreds of thousands of jobs were created, and Southern California, specifically Los Angeles and San Diego, cemented itself as one of the primary aircraft manufacturing locations in the United States.

California in the 1920s

While World War I helped boost California's economy during the 1910s, once the war was over, there was far less demand for the manufacturing of weapons, planes, and other military supplies. Factories and farms, which had expanded and hired thousands of extra workers, no longer had as large of demands, and many people were laid off as the companies attempted to downsize. The state's farmers, who had had massive demands during the war, were hit the hardest. That being said, the 1920s in the United States was a time of excessive spending. Over the course of the decade, automobile manufacturing became more commonplace, creating tens of thousands of jobs in the state as the demand for oil, street and highway construction, metals, and other automobile-related industries grew. The introduction of the car in the average American household is what would facilitate mass immigration to California over the course of the 1920s, as well as the following decades, seeing as settlers were no longer dependent on the railways. California's mass immigration came not only from within the United States but also from Asia, specifically the Philippines, during the 1920s. Although this boost in population and in tourism was encouraged during the twenties, as it became necessary for the growth of California's businesses and economy, it would become a matter of mass contention and dissatisfaction over the next decade when unemployment would reach an all-time high and Californians would feel their jobs were being stolen by immigrants.

Overall, the 1920s, in not only California but the rest of the United States as well, demonstrates exactly how divided the population truly was. While the twenties were a time of excess and partying for many, the rest of the population was socially and economically struggling. As the men returned from war and the farming sector of the economy suffered, the reunited families helped boost the urban population in California. Seeing as so many had returned from the horrors of war, the Roaring Twenties, as they are called, became about consumption, partying, and liberation for some. In the early 1900s, women had pushed for their right to vote, which they were finally granted in 1911. During World War I, women were granted another progressive liberty, the right to work, which became necessary as more and more men went off to war. Although women would not become common in the workforce until World War II, the 1910s and 1920s still represent a period of liberation for women of California and of the United States.

However, the twenties, which is often regarded as a period of liberation for many, was not a period of liberation for all. African Americans in California were considered to be second-class citizens, and although not officially segregated, African Americans, along with Native Americans, Mexicans, Chinese, and other racial minorities, were not allowed to attend white schools. While the civil rights movement grew in California, especially in Oakland, lynchings were still common occurrences, and Californians remained generally hostile to African Americans, even those who had fought alongside white American soldiers in World War I. Attitudes were not much better to the Asian population, and once again, the Asian minorities were resented for "stealing" Californian jobs, seeing as they were "willing" (forced) to work for less pay on farms. The racial tensions between California's Asian and white communities would continue to grow, especially in rural areas, which became apparent in the many violent clashes that would occur over the next decades, such as the 1936 Salinas Lettuce Strike.

The Great Depression

By 1940, the population of California would grow to 6,907,387, a growth of over four and a half million people from 1910. One of the greatest causes for mass immigration in the first few decades of the 20th century was the Great Depression. In October of 1929, on a day that has come to be known as Black Tuesday, the United States stock market crashed, affecting just about everyone in the country. People stopped buying products, businesses started laying off employees, families lost their homes, and while all this was happening, America endured one of its worst periods of drought at that point, another natural occurrence that northeasterners were not prepared for when they moved to California and other southern states. Californian farms suffered, and essentially all building and expansion projects were put on hold as the country tried to recover. Despite this, people continued to move to California. With idyllic movie scenes and paintings of the state in their minds, Americans flocked by the hundreds of thousands to hopefully find refuge in California. As seen in John Steinbeck's famous 1937 novel *Of Mice and Men* and his 1939 novel *The Grapes of Wrath*, immigrants arrived in California looking for work and essentially lived like nomads, moving from farm to farm as odd jobs arose.

However, as more and more immigrants arrived seeking a better life in California, the job market became smaller and smaller, especially since businesses continued to close down and lay off workers. Similar to their reaction to the Chinese laborers, the Californians quickly grew resentful of the American immigrants who were arriving in California and taking their jobs. In general, during the 20th century, California's class disparities became increasingly apparent as disasters occurred, such as the San Francisco earthquake or the Great Depression. By 1934, around a fifth of the population had to go on public relief to stay afloat. Immigrants continued to arrive, and since they were unestablished in the area, they were willing to migrate for jobs, which was not really a possibility for those who had established lives in California with families and homes. Once again, the percentage of the population who were homeless skyrocketed, and areas such as Oakland's Pipe City, where the unemployed lived in above-ground concrete sewer pipes, sprung up all over the state.

Political Reforms

After the disastrous events that plagued California's early history, such as the San Francisco earthquake and the Great Depression, the state's political system was put to the test and was eventually forced to change. Until the 20th century, California remained mostly relaxed about politics, seeing as the cities were mostly under the power of the businessmen. Californians seemed to share the common belief that "the best government was the least government." However, after the San Francisco earthquake, when the elite businessmen-run political parties failed the working class in the city, and when many civilians in California lost their jobs during the Great Depression, the state had an overwhelming need for a progressive and effective government. Although California had made some progressive political moves previously, such as the installation of the Workmen's Compensation, Insurance and Safety Act in 1913, the first real political reforms in California truly occurred in Washington, when President Franklin D. Roosevelt stepped in during the Great Depression and helped to regulate the economy. However, even with the installation of public relief, the population of California was not satisfied with their leaders, and the social unrest only grew with the arrival of immigrants taking Californian jobs during the Great Depression. Although the political unrest had been growing since the start of the century, the resentment culminated in the 1930s when violent worker protests and strikes broke out across the state, with one of the worst clashes being "Bloody Thursday," also known as the San Francisco General Strike of 1934.

Although there were protests and strikes by the unemployed, the employed population of California was not pleased with their conditions either. Those who did work worked excessively long hours in horrible conditions for poor pay, and during the Great Depression, employees had had enough and began to form and join unions to take action. The San Francisco General Strike of 1934 began after Harry Bridges, the founder and leader of the International Longshoremen's Association (ILA) labor union, led the dissatisfied workers in their labor strike on May 9th, 1934. This strike would inspire dozens of other large unions to gather along the Pacific coast and throughout the rest of California. After a little less than two months of striking, tensions escalated as the shipping companies refused to cooperate with the ILA's demands of better working conditions and wages. Finally, on July 5th, 1934, the dissatisfaction of the city of San Francisco, the striking members of the ILA, and the shipping companies culminated in a bloody clash, which would result in the injuries of dozens of men on both sides and the deaths of two. The event on July 5th, 1934, which came to be known as "Bloody Thursday," put an end to the ILA's strike, for the shipping companies gave in to their demands. The results of the ILA's strike inspired almost all of the employees in the San Francisco Bay Area to strike for their own rights, and the city was almost entirely shut down by striking employees for four days. The businesses in the Bay Area finally gave in to the requests of their employees, and the employees were aware that although their requests were met, working conditions during the Great Depression were still bad. As a result, they formed unions and threatened strikes when necessary.

Yet, despite the poor working conditions being slightly improved upon during the Great Depression, California's politics remained somewhat of a mess. Although the state was in disarray, millions were unemployed, and hundreds of thousands were homeless, Californian leaders somewhat frivolously spent the state's money to put California on the global map and set up the state's economy for the future. In 1932, the city of Los Angeles held the Olympics in its stadium, which had been built in the previous decade. The over-the-top Olympics celebrations that we know of today are accredited to being birthed in the 1932 Los Angeles Olympics, where the city set the present-day standard for the opening ceremonies, extensive facilities for the athletes, and the entire artistry of the event. In the words of journalist Westbrook Pegler, "I came to chronicle sports biggest disaster, I am leaving to describe its greatest triumph." The following year, the construction began on the San Francisco–Oakland Bay Bridge and the iconic Golden Gate Bridge. Over the course of the 1930s, a number of California's most important and iconic infrastructures were constructed, including the iconic Coit Tower and the Hoover Dam. The latter would not only provide clean drinking water but also allow the state to harvest hydroelectric energy.

Although the country looked up to Presidents Herbert Hoover, to some degree, and Franklin D. Roosevelt during and after the years of the Great Depression, Californians had no political force within their own state to look to for relief during the difficult years. While the Democratic Party improved its standing in the state over the course of the early 20th century, the Republican Party was still by far the popular choice; some of this may be attributed to the parties slowly changing platforms over the years. In 1930, the state elected Republican James Rolph Jr. (known as "Sunny Jim") as governor of California, and although he had served as the mayor of San Francisco during the years of 1912 to 1931, he was not at all prepared for his role as the state's leader during the country's worst economic period to date. Governor Rolph quickly lost popularity, and by the end of the decade, California would elect its first Democratic governor of the 20th century. Following James Rolph's successor, Frank Merriam, until the present day, the position of governor of California would swing back and forth between Republican and Democratic candidates. As of this writing, ever since James Rolph, California has not had three separate governors from the same party in a row, which just showcases the instability of California's politics, something that truly began during the Great Depression.

Overall, the state of California was in a strange state of affairs at the start of the 20th century. After years of mass immigration following the expansion of the railroads, the state endured a number of social and natural disasters, which left the civilians in a state of disorder. Although the working class, specifically the minority working class, in California never had it easy, the disparity between the rich elite and the poor working class became more and more apparent, and the public resentment finally culminated through strikes and riots.

World War II

When World War II began in 1939, the United States was reluctant to enter, seeing as they were still suffering from the effects of the Great Depression and it had not been long since World War I. This was especially true in California, which had become somewhat of a sleepy state, with unemployment at an all-time high. However, gradually, it seemed that the United States joining the war was all but inevitable. Still, Californians were reluctant to join yet again another devastating war, but this attitude would change on December 7th, 1941, due to the attack on Pearl Harbor. Seeing as Pearl Harbor was only around 2,500 miles away from Los Angeles, the people of California felt the urge to protect their country and family, and over the course of the next months, California became a fully-fledged participant in the Ally war efforts. Just as the Gold Rush had been close to a century ago, World War II was a wake-up call for California's population and economy. Similar to its reaction during World War I, California focused much of its attention on airplane manufacturing, although other weaponry manufacturing industries opened in the state as well. Farms, factories, and shipyards expanded and were suddenly in need of thousands of laborers, which very quickly put an end to the high rates of unemployment that had plagued the state and the country since the Great Depression. Although more than 800,000 Californian men would join the United States military and fight overseas, millions would be trained in Californian military institutions, meaning that, once again, the state's main contribution to the war would not be in men but in supplies, training facilities, food, and weaponry.

Although World War I had created California's aircraft industry, there had been almost no demand for Californian aircraft during the Great Depression. The start of World War II would force monumental growth in the industry. Californians designed, manufactured, and assembled everything from large bomber planes to small, fast fighter planes, injecting millions of dollars into the previously struggling economy. Alongside the aircraft industry, general technological advancements were made, such as radar, radio, and computer development, which would give birth to the state's soon-to-explode technological industry. On top of technology, the war gave a boost to the state's fields and farms, which had essentially died out during the previous decade. By the end of the war, California would actually contribute more food and other general war supplies (weapons, tech, aircraft, etc.) to the United States and Ally military than any other state in the country.

During the war, as the need for employees grew in the ever-growing aircraft, farming, and weapon manufacturing industries, the positions would not only be filled by the state's women but also by over a million Americans who had quickly immigrated to California in search of employment. Although California's population had been growing since the Gold Rush, there would be no greater boost in population since the Gold Rush than during World War II. Between

1940 and 1942, the state's population would increase by nearly a million people, and by 1950, the total population had grown to 10,677,000, an increase of more than 3.7 million people within the decade. World War II essentially skyrocketed the state's advancement toward the future, advancing its farming industry and shifting its economy toward technology development and manufacturing.

World War II represented a time of many social struggles and reforms for the various groups in California. Likely the group most affected by the Second World War was the Japanese, who represented quite a small population in California in the 1940s. The Japanese population had arrived in California mostly during the start of the 20th century to replace the Chinese on farms when anti-Chinese rhetoric became increasingly popular. Similar to the Chinese, the Japanese laborers had experienced prejudice and resentment from white Californians unable to find work during the early 20th century. However, hostility toward the Japanese Americans truly worsened at the start of the Second World War when Japan sided with the Axis. Following the Japanese attack on Pearl Harbor, Americans' opinion toward the Japanese people worsened, mostly due to media fear-mongering, and by the end of World War II, the United States had imprisoned around 112,000 Japanese Americans, many of whom had been living in the country for many decades. The prisoners were not only men but also women and children as well, and seeing as California contained around 74 percent of the Japanese population in the United States, most of the internment camps were located in the state of California itself. Following the events of Pearl Harbor, it would take decades until the intense fearful American racism against the Japanese Americans would lighten, and the United States would not actually issue an apology for its treatment of Japanese Americans during World War II until the 1980s. Within the 1940s, the Japanese American population in California would decrease by more than

10,000, and the Japanese would not feel safe enough to return to California until the following decade.

Another group who faced racism in California during the Second World War was the African Americans, many of whom had migrated to California as the state's industries boomed and the need for laborers was in demand. Although prejudice in California was not as pervasive as in other southern states in America, the black population in California was still subjected to serious racism, segregation, prejudice, and violence. The conditions the African American population was forced to endure through the war would inspire much of the civil rights movement, which would gain momentum over the next decade.

While many racial minorities continued to experience racism over the course of the Second World War, other groups managed to achieve social reforms and gain liberties. Similar to during World War I, with masses of Californian men joining the military in World War II, women were allowed and encouraged to join the workforce. During World War II, women took up jobs in the various expanding industries. However, once again, just as it had in World War I, the reforms would only last so long. When the men returned from war, women who had helped to carry the country's economy during the soldiers' absence were encouraged to quit their jobs and return to being traditional housewives, which would help fuel feminism and the women's rights movement, which would grow astronomically over the subsequent decades.

The Effects of World War II

In 1945, the war came to a close, and although 26,019 Californians who served in World War II had lost their lives, over 800,000 returned home, tired and in need of rehabilitation. By 1947, more than half of the veterans, or GIs as they came to be known, were still unemployed, and alongside hundreds of thousands more, they claimed unemployment benefits to stay afloat. Although California's market had been massively helped by the Second World War, which helped the state recover from the effects of the Great Depression, California had the second highest veteran unemployment rate in the United States. Despite the struggles veterans faced upon their return to California, they were much better off than soldiers who had returned from battles before the Second World War. This was due to the 1944 GI Bill of Rights. The GI Bill not only aided veterans (GIs) who were unemployed but also helped them find and pay for homes and land, medical attention, and education. With the GI Bill encouraging veterans to return to school, Californian post-secondary schools, which at that point had not been well established, saw massive growth in students, which allowed the universities and colleges to build larger campuses throughout California.

California's veterans were not the only ones who struggled to find employment during the 1950s. Though World War II helped grow the state's economy, once it was over and the demands for tech, aircraft, and manufacturing were no longer as urgent, the Californian economy entered into a period of depression. The year after the war had ended, California's unemployment rate was just under 9 percent, which was incredibly high in comparison to the United States' average of 3.9 percent. Overall, the main reason for the high unemployment rate was the constant growth in California's population over the course of the 20th century, which had not stopped in the years during or after the Second World War. Between 1945 and 1950, California's population would grow by more than one million people, meaning from the start of the war in 1939 to 1950, California's population increased by nearly four million people. Some of this immigration was due to the fact that millions of soldiers returned to the United States through California's de-embarkation centers. The United Nations also first met in San Francisco at the Opera House. This allowed thousands upon thousands of veterans to get a taste of California, many of whom would promptly decide to make the state their home. Overall, there were just not enough jobs for the ever-growing population, as well as for the returning military and the women who had been employed during World War II, some of whom wanted to keep their jobs.

Despite the first few years after the war being rather shaky for Californians, both those who had remained in the state and those who had recently returned, the economy quickly recovered and adjusted to the United States entering the Cold War. The effects of the Second World War were comparable to those of the Gold Rush. Throughout the late 1940s and 1950s, the economy continued to establish itself and prosper, while the population gradually grew, which brought upon a number of social movements, reforms, and changes.

California in the 1950s

In the words of Earl Warren, who was the governor of California between 1943 to 1953, "The war has caused us to actually jump into our future." Although California's wartime industries had very low demand in the first years following the Second World War, by 1947, America's need for weaponry, technology, and aircraft returned as the country entered the Cold War. By the end of the 1950s, more than three million people in the state worked in jobs related to Cold War defense, and Southern California became the United States' number one aircraft manufacturer.

During the 1950s, jobs were not as much of an issue as homes, which the state was seriously lacking in. Until this point, the urban population was entirely concentrated in a few cities, so the rural regions of California remained mostly undeveloped. However, this would no longer do for California's massive population. In the years following World War II, California's cities sprawled outward in all directions in a way they had not before, and the city suburbs, lined with simple, quick-built homes, were created to accommodate the masses looking to settle. Alongside the creation of the suburbs came the creation of the middle class, which had previously existed in California; however, for the most part, California was mostly split into the poor and the elite rich until the end of the Second World War. Although the middle class prospered in the suburbs, the vast majority of the working middle class were still employed in the cities, meaning they needed a stable form of transportation to get to and from work every day. Thus, in the 1950s, automobile ownership skyrocketed, as did consumerism in general. Middle-class families spent excessively on products that they could not have ever dreamed of owning before the war, such as dishwashers. By the 1960s, over 80 percent of the United States population owned a television, which had been a luxury item in the decades following its creation. As the middle class consumed, California's economy prospered, and the hundreds of new factories in the newly created product-manufacturing industries created jobs in the city for the unemployed. Thus, it became common for the poorer civilians in the United States to flock toward the cities from the rural areas, where the majority of the lower class had previously lived. Living in the city meant cars were not necessary, jobs were available, and homes were older and therefore cheaper. As the urban population sprawled into the suburbs, the newly settled middle-class population sought jobs, schools, shopping areas, and, of course, roads, in and around their immediate area, which also boosted the construction materials industry and construction employment sector. Overall, the state's economy not only recovered within the years following the Second World War but also grew astronomically, making California one of the wealthiest states in the country and one of the wealthiest regions in the world.

However, once again, this image of California's successes in the years subsequent to World War II fails to include the entirety of the state, and although the state of California did get wealthier, this wealth really only reached those who already had privileges before the war began. While it is true that over a third of California's women were employed in the decade following the Second World War, this was not, for the most part, because women wanted to be employed but because they were from a poorer family that could not live off the wage of the husband alone. This was especially common for recent immigrants and racial minorities, who struggled to achieve upward mobility amongst white Americans. One group who suffered from this was the Latin American population. As California's economy exploded in the 1950s, both the rich and the poor flocked away from the rural areas, where farms were still in need of workers. This led the United States to create the Bracero Program, which encouraged and facilitated over 200,000 Latin Americans, mostly from Mexico, to move to the United States and work on the farms, which generally offered lower and less secure pay than the booming industries in the cities. On top of only having work seasonally and working long hours for little pay, the Latin Americans were met with prejudice, discrimination, and sometimes violence from Californian farm owners, who knew they could get away with just about anything as the laborers needed the work. Although the Bracero Program ended in 1964, there are still to this day hundreds of thousands of Latin American laborers being underpaid and mistreated on Californian and American farms. Although the Latin Americans who arrived through the Bracero Program helped reestablish and fuel California's farming industry, they were not technically citizens of California, and if the growing season was poor and the farm needed fewer laborers that year, the Latin Americans, who had often established themselves in California with their working visas, were forced to return to their previous home. The laborers who wanted to stay in California could obtain a visa after having worked in the state for a set amount of years, but the road to obtaining a visa was difficult, and even if they earned citizenship, upward mobility was just as difficult.

The situation was also still difficult for the African American community in California, although it was improving. In the 1950s, the civil rights movement, with Martin Luther King Jr. as one of its figureheads, started making progress in improving the situation for every racial minority in all of America. Over the course of the mid-1950s, there were boycotts, rallies, and protests that finally called attention to the need for change. Although Mexican Americans had begun to desegregate Californian schools back in the 1940s, it would not be until 1955 that the United States would officially vote to desegregate schools. The desegregation of the housing market soon followed, allowing African Americans and other racial minorities in California and the rest of the United States to have the chance to purchase property in up-and-coming areas, attend better schools, and move upward in society, which had been almost entirely limited by government restrictions until that point. Although the years following the war were not great for all, many groups, including racial minorities, the LGBTQ community, and women, who had all previously suffered in California, began to make strides toward earning some liberties and respect.

Social Reforms in the 1960s and 1970s

If the 1950s in California represented a period of astronomical economic growth and the beginning of social reforms, the 1960s and 1970s represented a period of astronomical social change and development. Until the 1930s, California had been almost entirely Republican, and even as racial minorities immigrated to the state and social reforms were set in motion, the population remained quite traditional and right-leaning in their opinions. Though California would vote in its first Democratic governor in 1939 and numerous liberation movements would take shape in the years during and after the Second World War, it would not be until the 1960s that the state would become more left-leaning and Democratic. It would not be until the 1990s that California would become mainly Democratic, and it remains so to this day. In many ways, these political changes had been brewing since the dawn of the 20th century, yet the true breeding ground of the left-leaning ideas, which would be spread throughout the state over the course of the next decades, was California's post-secondary schools. During the 20th century, the percentage of the population who had or planned to attend university or college increased dramatically, especially thanks to the educational financial aid granted to soldiers who returned from World War II. Until the 1960s, higher education was mostly reserved for those who had the privilege to go, but that was about to change. In the 1960s, the postwar children who had been born in the homes of the suburban middle class had become young adults, and with the privilege of not having to work, university became a common next step for all twenty-something-year-olds looking to meet people their age rather than a luxury for those looking to join the workforce or seeking to expand their education. Quickly, California's universities had evolved to become a place to meet friends, party, join clubs, and, perhaps most of all, expand one's mind to the social reforms needed to make the country a better place for everyone. In the 1960s, at almost all of the California universities but most notably at the University of California at Berkeley, students shared and spread liberal left-leaning ideas, which led to student demonstrations. Over the course of the 1960s and 1970s, UC Berkeley and other California universities would be a leading force in the civil rights movement, the free speech movement, and the women's rights movement. They engaged in LGBTQ and Vietnam War protests, rallies, and demonstrations as well, helping to set in motion numerous social reforms and spread liberal ideas throughout the state.

The universities in California also helped set the precedent of the United States' budding cultural movements. In the years following World War II, California would become an epicenter of almost every cultural movement. Los Angeles developed into not only a city for films but also for music, and the city helped establish many musical icons. San Francisco would have its famous Summer of Love, a hippie movement, which forced the country to reflect on its attitude toward relationships, drugs, and art. In the 1960s and 1970s, California inherited close to eight million immigrants who arrived from all over the world, but unlike in the past, people were not arriving to strike it rich or buy property and start a new life. Instead, people were arriving to join in on the cultural movements that were taking place.

California in the 1980s and 1990s

The population growth brought by California's social movements in the 1960s and 1970s, which carried on into the 1980s, was especially obvious in the smaller Californian cities with universities. Students arrived from all over the country to study in California's universities, which had become somewhat of a dream for politically interested and liberal-minded students, many of which remained in the state after graduating. San Diego, which in 1950 had a population of only 333,865, ended up receiving a large portion of the college graduates, and the population grew to over a million people by 1990.

The 1980s would also represent a period of many social reforms for nearly every group in California, much of which had been brought on by the work of the students from the 1960s and 1970s. In the 1980s, for the first time in many years, the Native American population in California would significantly increase, as would the populations of almost all of the state's ethnic minorities due to the increase of foreign immigration. As California earned its left-leaning, liberal reputation, millions flocked to the open-minded cities. This can be seen, for example, in San Francisco with the growth of the LGBTQ community, as this city quickly became known as the most gay-friendly city in America.

Yet, even though the end of the 20th century would mark California's most accepting, aware, and open-minded period to date, things were far from solved. Despite all of the successes by the various movements in the 1960s and 1970s, the state's prejudice problems were not solved, and racism continued, resulting in violent protests and rallies. The LGBTQ community also suffered during the 1980s and 1990s, but their primary issue was no longer discrimination and violence but AIDS, which would not only kill thousands of young LGBTQ people but also hurt the LGBTQ's reputation, as civilians became fearful of them.

California's technological industry, which had essentially been created during World War II, boomed during the 1980s' digital revolution. By the 1980s, California's businesses had almost entirely relocated from San Francisco to Southern California. That being said, Northern California's budding Silicon Valley, located around San Jose, would soon become the tech and start-up capital of the United States. However, after years of almost entirely uninterrupted economic growth, the late 1980s and early 1990s would mark the state's first financial recession since the period right after World War II. This financial recession actually affected much of the world, but there were two main reasons for the fiscal issues in California. Firstly, during the 1980s and 1990s, the state was plagued with droughts and other natural disasters, which impacted farming. Secondly, in 1991, the United States officially put an end to the Cold War, which meant California's tech, aircraft, and weaponry manufacturing industries were far less in demand.

Similar to the small recession that had occurred just after World War II, California recovered rather quickly from the 1980–1990 recession, and the years following the recession would represent massive accelerated growth in many industries and the state's economy as a whole. The main reason for California's quick recovery in the 1990s was the insane explosion in the world's high-technology sector, for which Silicon Valley very quickly became the hub. Although Silicon Valley had already established itself as a contender in the country's technological race with the inventions of the microchip by Intel in 1971 and the PC by Apple in 1977, its growth over the course of the 1990s would be unparalleled. This was mainly due to the widespread growth of the internet in the 1990s and the immigration of highly specialized foreigners who wanted to join in on the technological advancements in Silicon Valley. Silicon Valley would also become known as the capital of start-ups, as innovative, creative people moved to the area to start their companies. Silicon Valley would eventually hold most of the country's most notable and affluent companies, and present-day Silicon Valley contains Apple, Adobe, Facebook, Netflix, PayPal, and Tesla, to name a few. Thousands arrived in Silicon Valley, hoping to finance their next big idea, and investors, hoping to purchase a percentage of what could possibly become the next biggest company in the world, were more than willing to secure million-dollar contracts.

Chapter 10 – Present-Day California (2000–2021)

California's Economy in the 21ˢᵗ Century

The internet brought Silicon Valley, California, and the United States dramatic economic growth, similar to that of the Gold Rush, as the Nasdaq stock market index close to quadrupled in five years. Finally, after more than a decade of unprecedented growth, the stock market bubble burst in late 2002 and brought down hundreds if not thousands of the companies that had been started in California's Silicon Valley. At the start of the 21ˢᵗ century, California's economy was also plagued by the effects of 9/11 and energy issues that caused rolling blackouts, negatively impacting almost all of California's businesses. As it had before, California would rebuild its economy once again in the new millennium and establish itself as one of the most prosperous states in the United States. Although it would be affected by various global recessions, such as the one in 2008, California has maintained its position as the state with the highest GDP (gross domestic product) in the nation. That being said, by the 21ˢᵗ century, the division between the upper class and the middle and lower classes, which had always existed in California, had exponentially expanded. Although California is one of the richest states in the nation, the wealth is not distributed, and it is held almost entirely by the elites in the society, such as the Silicon Valley businessmen and the Hollywood Hills celebrities. In fact, California has one of the highest homeless populations in the United States.

California's Politics in the 21st Century

In 2003, Californians voted Arnold Schwarzenegger as their state governor, and although Schwarzenegger was not the first actor or celebrity in politics (most notably preceding him was President Ronald Regan), he was certainly a controversial pick. Even before Arnold Schwarzenegger was elected, much like Donald Trump, he had earned his place as a controversial celebrity with views that went against the liberal and Democratic scene in Hollywood. To many, Schwarzenegger represented a period of social regression, as he imposed laws that many felt directly hurt minority groups, such as when he and the California Supreme Court banned same-sex marriage in 2008. Overall, California is still far from perfect, and socially, it still has a way to go, but the state is considered to be far more accepting toward minority groups than other states in America. Following Schwarzenegger's terms, there has not been another Republican governor in California, as the state has become Democratic-leaning, which it had been gearing to become since the 1960s and 1970s.

Conclusion

California's development has always been completely dependent on its mass immigrations, which began with the forty-niners during the Gold Rush. As people came from all over the world to experience what they had heard about, read about, and eventually seen in the movies, few wanted to leave California's mild climate and beautiful landscapes. This was true during all of the mass immigrations surrounding the Gold Rush, the Great Depression, and World War II. Although the mass immigrations allowed California's economy to grow astronomically in only a few centuries, they were not without their problems. The state of California had long been inhabited by the first settlers of the region, who were continuously pushed out of their home as immigrants arrived. In fact, many native Californian tribes were actually relocated off of their ancestral land and out of the state entirely. Aside from the native Californians, the mass immigrants brought foreigners from just about

everywhere, such as Asia, the United States, South America, Europe, and more. Yet, despite the fact that California was stolen from the Native Americans, many of the groups who arrived over the course of the most recent centuries felt entitled to the land. At first, the Spanish caused the Native Americans to suffer. When the Republic of Mexico acquired Mexico, both the Native Americans and the Spanish suffered. When the United States acquired Mexico, all three of those groups suffered. During the Gold Rush, California received its first mass immigration, and although foreigners arrived from all over the world to try and strike it rich, the racial minorities, including the Mexicans and Native Americans, who had lived in California long before the Gold Rush, were resented by the white newcomers, as were other racial minorities, most notably the Asians, who arrived at the same time. With California's mass immigrations would come mass entitlement,

resentment, and social issues.

For many years, California remained quite similar to the other southern states, as it was quite traditional, segregated, and right-leaning by today's standards. However, over time, the racial minorities began to make up a majority, and before long, public opinion started to shift. With the widespread growth of universities and other post-secondary education schools in the 1960s and 1970s came the mass spread of information, and before long, California's universities became the home to almost every left-leaning social movement in the country. Students fought for women, LGBTQ, African American, and Asian rights, as well as many other issues. By the end of the 20th century, California had become a left-leaning state, and it eventually transitioned into the state we recognize today, a

predominantly Democratic liberal population. However, it still has many issues to face. For example, present-day California is the most populous and wealthy state in the country, yet the wealth is only in the hands of a select few, and the wealth gap and social prejudices are still very much in existence. Only time will tell if California continues to embrace its current liberal stance or if it will switch to a more conservative outlook, a pattern that can be seen throughout the state's history.

Here's another book by Captivating History that you might like

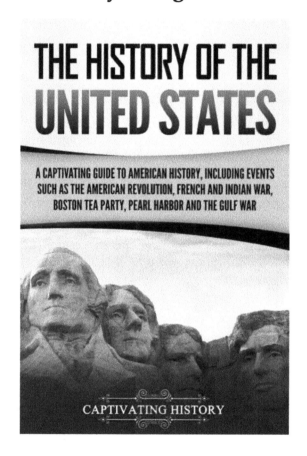

Free Bonus from Captivating History (Available for a Limited time)

Hi History Lovers!

Now you have a chance to join our exclusive history list so you can get your first history ebook for free as well as discounts and a potential to get more history books for free! Simply visit the link below to join.

Captivatinghistory.com/ebook

Also, make sure to follow us on Facebook, Twitter and Youtube by searching for Captivating History.

Bibliography

Alaska Public Land Information Centers. "How Close Is Alaska to Russia?" Your Guide to Experiencing Alaska's Public Lands. July 05, 2017. Accessed February 20, 2021. https://www.alaskacenters.gov/faqs-people-often-ask/how-close-alaska-russia.

Bacich, Damian, Dr. "Timeline: European Exploration and Settlement of California." The California Frontier Project. June 01, 2018. Accessed February 24, 2021. https://www.californiafrontier.net/timeline-european-exploration-settlement/.

Bacich, Damian, Dr. "Juan Bautista De Anza: Son of the Frontier." The California Frontier Project. September 30, 2020. Accessed February 24, 2021. https://www.californiafrontier.net/juan-bautista-de-anza-son-of-the-frontier/.

Britannica, The Editors of Encyclopedia. "Pomo." Encyclopedia Britannica. June 10, 2019. Accessed February 23, 2021. https://www.britannica.com/topic/Pomo-people.

Britannica, The Editors of Encyclopedia. "Chumash." Encyclopedia Britannica. May 24, 2019. Accessed February 23, 2021. https://www.britannica.com/topic/Chumash.

Britannica, The Editors of Encyclopedia. "Gold Rush." Encyclopedia Britannica. October 16, 2019. Accessed February 24, 2021. https://www.britannica.com/event/gold-rush.

Britannica, The Editors of Encyclopedia. "Hollywood." Encyclopedia Britannica. November 19, 2019. Accessed February 25, 2021. https://www.britannica.com/place/Hollywood-California.

Britannica, The Editors of Encyclopedia. "Miwok." Encyclopedia Britannica. April 8, 2020. Accessed February 23, 2021. https://www.britannica.com/topic/Miwok.

Britannica, The Editors of Encyclopedia. "Juan Rodríguez Cabrillo." Encyclopedia Britannica. March 9, 2020. Accessed February 23, 2021. https://www.britannica.com/biography/Juan-Rodriguez-Cabrillo.

Britannica, The Editors of Encyclopedia. "San Diego." Encyclopedia Britannica. May 7, 2020. Accessed February 24, 2021. https://www.britannica.com/place/San-Diego-California.

Britannica, The Editors of Encyclopedia. "St. Junípero Serra." Encyclopedia Britannica. November 20, 2020. Accessed February 24, 2021. https://www.britannica.com/biography/Saint-Junipero-Serra.

Britannica, The Editors of Encyclopedia. "Mexican-American War." Encyclopedia Britannica. November 10, 2020. Accessed February 24, 2021. https://www.britannica.com/event/Mexican-American-War.

Britannica, The Editors of Encyclopedia. "Bear Flag Revolt." Encyclopedia Britannica. February 14, 2020. Accessed February 24, 2021. https://www.britannica.com/event/Bear-Flag-Revolt.

Britannica, The Editors of Encyclopedia. "California Gold Rush." Encyclopedia Britannica. May 27, 2020. Accessed February 24, 2021. https://www.britannica.com/topic/California-Gold-Rush.

Britannica, The Editors of Encyclopedia. "San Francisco Earthquake of 1906." Encyclopedia Britannica. May 12, 2020. Accessed February 25, 2021. https://www.britannica.com/event/San-Francisco-earthquake-of-1906.

Britannica, The Editors of Encyclopedia. "Juan Ponce De León." Encyclopedia Britannica. January 01, 2021. Accessed February 24, 2021. https://www.britannica.com/biography/Juan-Ponce-de-Leon.

Britannica, The Editors of Encyclopedia. "John Sutter." Encyclopedia Britannica. February 12, 2021. Accessed February 24, 2021. https://www.britannica.com/biography/John-Sutter.

California Military History. "Proclamation of the Bear Flag Revolt." The Mexican War and California. June 23, 2017. Accessed February 24, 2021.

http://www.militarymuseum.org/BearFlagRevolt.html.

California Native American Heritage Commission. "Short Overview of California Indian History." California Indian History – California Native American Heritage Commission. 2021. Accessed February 18, 2021. http://nahc.ca.gov/resources/california-indian-history/.

California State Capitol Museum. "Called to Action: California's Role in WW2."

California Transformed. 2016. Accessed February 26, 2021.

http://www.capitolmuseum.ca.gov/special/ww2/introduction/california-transformed.

California State Parks. "Hernando de Alarcón Expedition." State of California. 2021.

Accessed February 24, 2021.

https://ohp.parks.ca.gov/ListedResources/Detail/568.

California State University. "Mexican California: The Heyday of the Ranchos." California History Online | The First Californians. 2021. Accessed February 24, 2021.

http://www.csun.edu/~sg4002/courses/417/readings/mexican.pdf.

California State University. "The Great Depression: California in the Thirties." CSUN. 2021. Accessed February 25, 2021.

http://www.csun.edu/~sg4002/courses/417/readings/depression.pdf.

Caryl-Sue, National Geographic Society. "Columbus Makes Landfall in the Caribbean." National Geographic Society. September 6, 2020. Accessed February 24, 2021.

https://www.nationalgeographic.org/thisday/oct12/columbus-makes-landfall-caribbean/.

De Portola Middle. "Who Is Gaspar de Portola?" We've Got History. 2021. Accessed February 24, 2021.

https://deportola.sandiegounified.org/about_us/who_is_gaspar_de_portola.

Defense Language Institute Foreign Language Center. "History of the Presidio of

Monterey." DLIFLC. 2021. Accessed February 24, 2021.

https://www.dliflc.edu/about/command-history/online-exhibit-history-of-the-presidio-of-monterey/.

Desert USA and Digital West Media, Inc. "Juan Bautista De Anza." Desert USA. 2020. Accessed February 24, 2021. https://www.desertusa.com/desert-people/juan-bautista-de-anza.html.

Fen Montaigne, Jennie Rothenberg Gritz. "The Story of How Humans Came to the Americas Is Constantly Evolving." Smithsonian.com. Jan. & Feb. 2020. Accessed February 18, 2021. https://www.smithsonianmag.com/science-nature/how-humans-came-to-americas-180973739/.

Frommer's. "History in California." Frommer's. 2021. Accessed February 26, 2021. https://www.frommers.com/destinations/california/in-depth/history.

Greshko, Michael. "Humans in California 130,000 Years Ago? Get the Facts." Culture. April 26, 2017. Accessed February 18, 2021. https://www.nationalgeographic.com/culture/article/mastodons-americas-peopling-migrations-archaeology-science.

History.com Editors. "Vasco Núñez De Balboa." History.com. August 21, 2018. Accessed February 24, 2021. https://www.history.com/topics/exploration/vasco-nunez-de-balboa.

History.com Editors. "Hollywood." History.com. March 27, 2018. Accessed February 25, 2021. https://www.history.com/topics/roaring-twenties/hollywood.

History.com Editors. "California Becomes the 31st State in Record Time." A&E Television Networks. September 9, 2020. Accessed February 24, 2021. https://www.history.com/this-day-in-history/california-becomes-the-31st-state-in-record-time.

Inda, Estella. "What's in a Name—California." San Jose Public Library. September 01, 2018. Accessed February 23, 2021. https://www.sjpl.org/blog/whats-name-california.

Innes, Ralph Hammond. "Hernán Cortés." Encyclopedia Britannica. January 07, 2021. Accessed February 24, 2021. https://www.britannica.com/biography/Hernan-Cortes.

Keen, Benjamin. "Vasco Núñez De Balboa." Encyclopedia Britannica. January 08, 2021. Accessed February 24, 2021. https://www.britannica.com/biography/Vasco-Nunez-de-Balboa.

Lonely Planet. "History of California." Lonely Planet. 2021. Accessed February 26, 2021.
https://www.lonelyplanet.com/usa/california/history#110261.

Los Angeles Almanac. "Pio Pico - Last Governor of Mexican California." Los Angeles Almanac. 2021. Accessed February 24, 2021.
http://www.laalmanac.com/history/hi05s.php.

MacroTrends. "California Population 1900–2020." MacroTrends. 2021. Accessed February 26, 2021.
https://www.macrotrends.net/states/california/population.

Martha Heasley Cox Center for Steinbeck Studies. "1920 to 1930: A Period of Extremes." 1920 to 1930 | Steinbeck in the Schools | San Jose State University. October 25, 2016. Accessed February 26, 2021.
https://sits.sjsu.edu/context/historical/hist_context_1920s/index.html.

Martha Heasley Cox Center for Steinbeck Studies. "1950–1960 Laying the Foundation." Steinbeck in the Schools | San Jose State University. October 25, 2016. Accessed February 26, 2021.
https://sits.sjsu.edu/context/historical/hist_context_1950s/index.html.

Martha Heasley Cox Center for Steinbeck Studies. "World War II Homefront." Steinbeck in the Schools | San Jose State University. October 25, 2016. Accessed February 26, 2021.
https://sits.sjsu.edu/context/historical/hist_context_1940s_homefront/index.html.

McNamee, Gregory Lewis, and Neil Morgan. "California." Encyclopedia Britannica. February 04, 2021. Accessed February 24, 2021.
https://www.britannica.com/place/California-state.

National Historic Trail. "Juan Bautista De Anza." Welcome to the Anza Historic Trail. 2021. Accessed February 24, 2021.
http://www.anzahistorictrail.org/.

National Park Service U.S Department of the Interior. "The Bering Land Bridge Theory." National Parks Service. January 29, 2021. Accessed February 20, 2021.
https://www.nps.gov/bela/learn/historyculture/the-bering-land-bridge-theory.htm.

National Parks Service. "Early History of the California Coast." National Parks Service. Accessed February 23, 2021.

https://www.nps.gov/nr/travel/ca/intro.htm#:˜:text=On September 28, 1542, Juan,land for thousands of years.

New World Encyclopedia. "Atsugewi." Atsugewi - New World Encyclopedia. April 26,

2016. Accessed February 21, 2021. https://www.newworldencyclopedia.org/entry/Atsugewi.

New World Encyclopedia. "Modoc People." Modoc People - New World Encyclopedia. October 12, 2018. Accessed February 21, 2021. https://www.newworldencyclopedia.org/entry/Modoc_people.

New World Encyclopedia. "Achomawi." Achomawi - New World Encyclopedia. November 3, 2019. Accessed February 21, 2021. https://www.newworldencyclopedia.org/entry/Achomawi.

O'Brien, Cynthia, and Jamie Kiffel Alcheh. "Native People of California." History. February 16, 2021. Accessed February 18, 2021. https://kids.nationalgeographic.com/history/article/native-people-of-california.

Oakland Museum of California. "Early Statehood: 1850–1880s: Federal Indian Policy & the Modoc War." Picture This. 2021. Accessed February 25, 2021. http://picturethis.museumca.org/timeline/early-statehood-1850-1880s/modoc-war/info.

Oakland Museum of California. "Progressive Era: 1890–1920s: Immigration Period of Restrictions." Picture This. 2021. Accessed February 25, 2021. http://picturethis.museumca.org/timeline/progressive-era-1890-1920s/immigration-period-restrictions/info.

Oakland Museum of California. "Early Statehood: 1850–1880s: Women's Rights." Picture This. 2021. Accessed February 25, 2021. http://picturethis.museumca.org/timeline/early-statehood-1850-1880s/womens-rights/info.

Oakland Museum of California. "Progressive Era: 1890–1920s: Effects of 1906 Earthquake." Picture This. 2021. Accessed February 25, 2021. http://picturethis.museumca.org/timeline/progressive-era-1890-1920s/effects-1906-earthquake/info.

Oakland Museum of California. "Depression Era: 1930s: Depression." Picture This. 2021. Accessed February 26, 2021. http://picturethis.museumca.org/timeline/depression-era-1930s/depression/info.

Oakland Museum of California. "Depression Era: 1930s: 'Bloody Thursday' & Other Labor Strikes." Picture This. 2021. Accessed February 26, 2021. http://picturethis.museumca.org/timeline/depression-era-1930s/political-protest/info.

Pastron, Otto. "California in WW1 - Then." United States Foundation for the Commemoration of the World Wars. 2021. Accessed February 26, 2021. https://www.worldwar1centennial.org/index.php/california-in-ww1-then.html.

PBS. "The West - Junipero Serra." Public Broadcasting Service. 2001. Accessed February 24, 2021. https://www.pbs.org/weta/thewest/people/s_z/serra.htm.

PBS American Experience. "Transcontinental Railroad Timeline." PBS. 2021. Accessed February 24, 2021. https://www.pbs.org/wgbh/americanexperience/features/tcrr-timeline/.

PBS American Experience. "Workers of the Central and Union Pacific Railroad." PBS. 2021. Accessed February 24, 2021. https://www.pbs.org/wgbh/americanexperience/features/tcrr-workers-central-union-pacific-railroad/.

Prine, Paul E., and Lowell John Bean. "California Indian." Encyclopedia Britannica. May 29, 2019. Accessed February 18, 2021. https://www.britannica.com/topic/California-Indian.

San Diego History Center. "Sebastián Vizcaíno." San Diego History Center: San Diego, CA: Our City, Our Story. 2021. Accessed February 24, 2021. https://sandiegohistory.org/archives/biographysubject/vizcaino/.

San Diego Tourism Authority. "History: San Diego's 250th Anniversary." History. November 21, 2019. Accessed February 24, 2021. https://sandiego250.com/history/.

Santa Cruz Museum of Natural History. "Virtual Exhibit: First Peoples of California." Santa Cruz Museum of Natural History.

November 03, 2020. Accessed February 18, 2021.
https://www.santacruzmuseum.org/first-peoples-of-california-virtual-exhibit/.

Smithsonian National Postal Museum. "Settlement of California." Settlement of California | National Postal Museum. 2021. Accessed February 24, 2021.
https://postalmuseum.si.edu/exhibition/celebrating-hispanic-heritage-growth-settlement-of-the-southwest/settlement-of-california.

Starr, Kevin. *California: A History.* Modern Library, 2007.

State of California. "The Civil War in California." California Department of Parks and Recreation. 2021. Accessed February 24, 2021.
https://www.parks.ca.gov/?page_id=26775.

Steen, Francis F. "Local California Chronology 2: The First European Contact." 2. The First European Contact. March 31, 2002. Accessed February 24, 2021.
http://cogweb.ucla.edu/Chumash/California_First_Europeans.html.

The American Battlefield Trust. "10 Facts: California during the Civil War." American Battlefield Trust. May 31, 2018. Accessed February 24, 2021. https://www.battlefields.org/learn/articles/10-facts-california-during-civil-war.

The American Oil & Gas Historical Society. "First California Oil Wells." American Oil & Gas Historical Society. September 07, 2020. Accessed February 25, 2021. https://www.aoghs.org/petroleum-pioneers/first-california-oil-well/.

The California Historical Society. "Meanwhile out West: Colonizing California, 1769–1821." California Historical Society. June 27, 2019. Accessed February 24, 2021.
https://californiahistoricalsociety.org/exhibitions/meanwhile-out-west-colonizing-california-1769-1821/.

The Library of Congress. "The First Peoples of California." California as I Saw It: First-Person Narratives of California's Early Years, 1849 to 1900. 2021. Accessed February 18, 2021.
https://www.loc.gov/collections/california-first-person-narratives/articles-and-essays/early-california-history/first-peoples-of-california/.

The Library of Congress. "Spanish California." California as I Saw It: First-Person Narratives of California's Early Years, 1849 to 1900. 2021. Accessed February 23, 2021. https://www.loc.gov/collections/california-first-person-narratives/articles-and-essays/early-california-history/spanish-california/.

The Library of Congress. "Mexican California: Early California History: An Overview: Articles and Essays." California as I Saw It: First-Person Narratives of California's Early Years, 1849-1900. 2021. Accessed February 24, 2021. https://www.loc.gov/collections/california-first-person-narratives/articles-and-essays/early-california-history/mexican-california/.

The Library of Congress. "The United States and California." California as I Saw It: First-Person Narratives of California's Early Years, 1849 to 1900. 2021. Accessed February 24, 2021. https://www.loc.gov/collections/california-first-person-narratives/articles-and-essays/early-california-history/united-states-and-california/.

The Library of Congress. "The Discovery of Gold." The Library of Congress. 2021. Accessed February 25, 2021. https://www.loc.gov/collections/california-first-person-narratives/articles-and-essays/early-california-history/discovery-of-gold/.

The Library of Congress. "The Mines." The Library of Congress. 2021. Accessed February 24, 2021. https://www.loc.gov/collections/california-first-person-narratives/articles-and-essays/early-california-history/mines/.

The Library of Congress. "Government and Law." The Library of Congress. 2021. Accessed February 24, 2021. https://www.loc.gov/collections/california-first-person-narratives/articles-and-essays/early-california-history/government-and-law/.

The Library of Congress. "From Gold Rush to Golden State." The Library of Congress. 2021. Accessed February 24, 2021. https://www.loc.gov/collections/california-first-person-narratives/articles-and-essays/early-california-history/from-gold-rush-to-golden-state/.

The Library of Congress. "California: Magnet for Tourists and Home Buyers." The Library of Congress. 2021. Accessed February 25, 2021.
https://www.loc.gov/collections/california-first-person-narratives/articles-and-essays/early-california-history/magnet-for-tourists-and-home-buyers/.

The Library of Congress. "Other Californians." The Library of Congress. 2021. Accessed February 25, 2021.
https://www.loc.gov/collections/california-first-person-narratives/articles-and-essays/early-california-history/other-californians/.

The Library of Congress. "The Turn of the Century in California." The Library of Congress. 2021. Accessed February 25, 2021.
https://www.loc.gov/collections/california-first-person-narratives/articles-and-essays/early-california-history/turn-of-the-century-in-california/.

The National Parks Service. "Five Views: An Ethnic Historic Site Survey for California (Japanese Americans)." U.S. Department of the Interior. November 17, 2004. Accessed February 26, 2021.
https://www.nps.gov/parkhistory/online_books/5views/5views4b.htm.

The National Parks Service. "National Park Service." National Parks Service. March 22, 2005. Accessed February 24, 2021.
https://www.nps.gov/parkhistory/online_books/explorers/sitee4.htm.

The National Parks Service. "California's Role in the Civil War." U.S. Department of the Interior. May 13, 2020. Accessed February 24, 2021.
https://www.nps.gov/goga/learn/historyculture/california-in-civil-war.htm.

The National Parks Service. "San Diego Mission Church (San Diego De Alcala)—Early History of the California Coast—A National Register of Historic Places Travel Itinerary." National Parks Service. 2021. Accessed February 24, 2021.
https://www.nps.gov/nr/travel/ca/ca3.htm.

U.S. Geological Survey. "The Great 1906 San Francisco Earthquake." U.S. Geological Survey. 2021. Accessed February 25, 2021.
https://earthquake.usgs.gov/earthquakes/events/1906calif/18april/.

Union Pacific. "Union Pacific History and Chronologies." Union Pacific. 2021. Accessed February 24, 2021. https://www.up.com/heritage/history/.

University of California. "San Francisco General Strike." Calisphere. 2005. Accessed February 25, 2021. https://calisphere.org/exhibitions/31/san-francisco-general-strike/.

University of Minnesota Libraries. "Sea Otter." The University of Minnesota Libraries. 2021. Accessed February 24, 2021. https://www.lib.umn.edu/bell/tradeproducts/seaotter.

University of Virginia. "'Free Labor' Ideology in the North." Virginia Center for Digital History. 2005. Accessed February 24, 2021. http://www.vcdh.virginia.edu/solguide/VUS06/essay06c.html.